50 Walks in
WARWICKSHIRE & WEST MIDLANDS

50 Walks of 2–10 Miles

Contents

The Walks

50 Walks in
WARWICKSHIRE &
WEST MIDLANDS

Produced by AA Publishing
© AA Media Limited 2013

First published 2001
Second edition 2008
New edition 2013

Published by AA Publishing (a trading name of AA Media Limited, whose registered office is Fanum House, Basing View, Basingstoke, Hampshire RG21 4EA; registered number 06112600)

Researched and written by Andrew Noyce
Field checked and updated 2012 by Madge Cairns, Martin Cairns, Chris Bagshow, Vivienne Crow and Martin Andrew

Series Management: Karen Rigden
Editor: Ann F Stonehouse
Designer: Tracey Butler
Proofreader: Sheila Hawkins Ltd
Digtial imaging & repro: Jacqueline Street
Production: Richard Firth
Cartography provided by the Mapping Services Department of AA Publishing

Printed and bound in the UK by Butler Tanner & Dennis

Mapping in this book is derived from the following products:
OS Landranger 139 (walks 1–6, 15, 16, 20, 22, 26, 27, 30)
OS Landranger 140 (walks 27, 30, 31, 35, 38–39, 42, 45, 47, 50)
OS Landranger 150 (walks 11–14)
OS Landranger 151 (walks 13–14, 18–19, 25, 28–29, 32–34, 36, 37, 41, 43–49)
OS Landranger 163 (walk 36)
OS Landranger 164 (walk 36)
OS Explorer 205 (walks 17, 23–24)
OS Explorer 220 (walks 7, 8–9)
OS Explorer 232 (walk 21)
© Crown Copyright and database rights 2013. 100021153.

A04976

ISBN: 978-0-7495-7407-9
ISBN (SS): 978-0-7495-7445-1

A CIP catalogue record for this book is available from the British Library.

The Automobile Association wishes to thank the following photographers and organisations for their assistance in the preparation of this book.
Abbreviations for the picture credits are as follows – (AA) AA World Travel Library
3 AA/C Jones; 9 AA/C Jones; 10 AA/C Jones; 12/13 AA/C Jones; 20/21 AA/C Jones; 42/43 AA/C Jones; 50/51 AA/C Jones; 74/75 AA/C Jones; 84 AA/H Palmer; 94/95 AA/C Jones; 107 AA/C Jones; 113 AA/C Jones; 130/131 AA/C Jones; 142/143 AA/C Jones.

Right: A frosty path on Wychbury Hill, Pedmore

Following the Walks

An information panel for each walk shows its relative difficulty, the distance and total amount of ascent. An indication of the gradients you will encounter is shown by the rating ▲▲▲ (no steep slopes) to ▲▲▲ (several very steep slopes). Each walk is rated for its relative difficulty compared to the other walks in this book. Walks marked +++ and colour-coded green are likely to be shorter and easier with little total ascent. Those marked with +++ and colour-coded orange are of intermediate difficultly. The hardest walks are marked +++ and colour-coded red.

MAPS

There are 40 maps, covering the 50 walks. Some walks have a suggested option in the same area. The information panel for these walks will tell you how much extra walking is involved. On short-cut suggestions the panel will tell you the total distance if you set out from the start of the main walk. Where an option returns to the same point on the main walk, just the distance of the loop is given. Where an option leaves the main walk at one point and returns to it at another, then the distance shown is for the whole walk. The minimum time suggested is for reasonably fit walkers and doesn't allow for stops. Each walk has a suggested map.

ROUTE MAP LEGEND

_ _ _→_ _	Walk Route	▢	Built-up Area
❶	Route Waypoint	▢	Woodland Area
– – – –	Adjoining Path	👥	Toilet
＼|/	Viewpoint	P	Car Park
•	Place of Interest	⊞	Picnic Area
⌂	Steep Section	)(	Bridge

START POINTS

The start of each walk is given as a six-figure grid reference prefixed by two letters indicating which 100km square of the National Grid it refers to. You'll find more information on grid references on most Ordnance Survey maps.

DOGS

We have tried to give dog owners useful advice about how dog friendly each walk is. Please respect other countryside users. Keep your dog under control, especially around livestock, and obey local bylaws and other dog control notices.

CAR PARKING

Many of the car parks suggested are public, but occasionally you may find you have to park on the roadside or in a lay-by. Please be considerate when you leave your car, ensuring that access roads or gates are not blocked and that other vehicles can pass safely.

WALKS LOCATOR

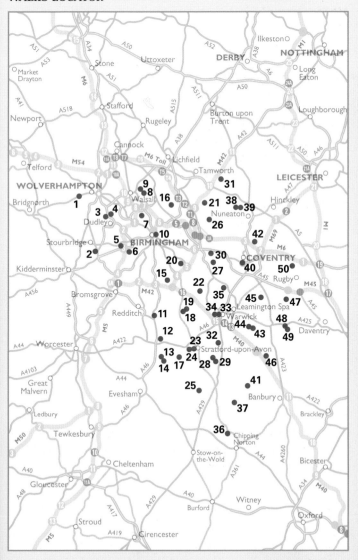

Walking in Warwickshire and the West Midlands

The sparkle of early morning sunlight on a country river as it meanders through beautiful countryside; the reflections of sailing boats on a country lake; relaxing with a pint in the garden of an old English pub in a picturesque village; the sight of colourful narrow boats making their way through a flight of lock gates; the visual impact created by an historic castle. These are just a few of the experiences that can be enjoyed in Warwickshire and the West Midlands. These two counties form the picturesque and historic Heart of England, and an ancient cross in the village of Meriden supposedly marks the spot regarded as the very centre of England. There may be few seriously high hills in this fertile plain, but it is an area full of attractive walking in rolling countryside, blessed with a fascinating history and many wonderful places and buildings to visit.

Warwickshire is Shakespeare's county, and the footprint of the famous Bard appears almost everywhere. The West Midlands is dominated by the great industrial city of Birmingham and embraces the Black Country, a region whose limitless energy has helped shape the destiny of Britain.

William Shakespeare is probably the most famous playwright the world has known. He was born and brought up around the beautiful Warwickshire town of Stratford-upon-Avon, and many of his plays draw upon his own experiences in the area. In his youth, Stratford was an important market town and this gave Shakespeare the opportunity to note the manners, dress and speech of the tradesmen, farmers, milkmaids, lawyers and others who attended on market day. Stratford was a centre of government and rural business matters, with one of the finest grammar schools in the country. Today the swans gather by Clopton Bridge to be fed by the tourists who come to visit the home of the Bard.

Warwickshire has a history that embraces the Civil War, and many castles and large country houses are scattered over the county. Warwick Castle is the home of the Earl of Warwick; Kenilworth Castle was a stronghold for lords and kings of England in the 11th and 12th centuries; Ragley Hall is the home of Lord Hertford; Coughton Court is the home of the Throckmorton family and history connects it with the Gunpowder Plot; Baddesley Clinton Manor House contains a number of priests' holes used to hide the clergy from Cromwell's men; Packwood House has a garden of yew trees that represent Christ, the four evangelists, the apostles and the multitude at the sermon on the mount; Upton House is a fine

Right: A peacock in the gardens at Warwick Castle

William and Mary mansion; Compton Wynyates is one of the most beautiful Tudor houses in the country; and Charlecote House is where Shakespeare is said to have been caught poaching deer.

The West Midlands was central to Britain's development during the Industrial Revolution. Canals were built to transport coal, ironware, glass, pottery and textiles across the country, and it remains a vibrant area of business. Today there are fine parkland areas intermixed with the urban sprawl, and many preserved historic sites to discover. So enjoy a little of everything as you explore these central regions of England on foot.

PUBLIC TRANSPORT Either the start points of the walks or the villages en route are within easy reach using public transport. Walks 2, 3, 4, 10, 15, 16, 18, 19, 20, 23, 24, 31, 33, 34, 40 and 42 all start close to railway stations. For train times call the 24-hour national train information line 08457 48 49 50 or go online to www.nationalrail.co.uk. For times of buses and leaflets/maps of public transport routes call Traveline 0871 200 22 33. Their website (www.traveline.org.uk) has maps with a list of train stations across Warwickshire and the West Midlands. Alternatively, plan your journey at www.transportdirect.info.

Above: A tranquil lake at Chesterton, near Harbury

Walking in Safety

All these walks are suitable for any reasonably fit person, but less experienced walkers should try the easier walks first. Route finding is usually straightforward, but you will find that an Ordnance Survey or AA map is a useful addition to the route maps and descriptions.

RISKS

Although each walk here has been researched with a view to minimising the risks to the walkers who follow its route, no walk in the countryside can be considered to be completely free from risk. Walking in the outdoors will always require a degree of common sense and judgement to ensure that it is as safe as possible.

- Be particularly careful on cliff paths and in upland terrain, where the consequences of a slip can be very serious.
- Remember to check tidal conditions before walking on the seashore.
- Some sections of route are by, or cross, busy roads. Take care and remember traffic is a danger even on minor country lanes.
- Be careful around farmyard machinery and livestock, especially if you have children with you.
- Be aware of the consequences of changes in the weather and check the forecast before you set out. Carry spare clothing and a torch if you are walking in the winter months. Remember the weather can change very quickly at any time of the year, and in moorland and heathland areas, mist and fog can make route finding much harder. Don't set out in these conditions unless you are confident of your navigation skills in poor visibility. In summer remember to take account of the heat and sun; wear a hat and carry spare water.
- On walks away from centres of population you should carry a whistle and survival bag. If you do have an accident requiring the emergency services, make a note of your position as accurately as possible and dial 999.

COUNTRYSIDE CODE

- Be safe, plan ahead and follow any signs.
- Leave gates and property as you find them.
- Protect plants and animals and take your litter home.
- Keep dogs under close control.
- Consider other people.

For more information visit www.naturalengland.org.uk/ourwork/enjoying/countrysidecode

Overleaf: A cluster of narrowboats at Birmingham's Gas Street Basin

Along the Staffordshire & Worcestershire Canal

DISTANCE 4.5 miles (7.2km)	MINIMUM TIME 1hr 30min

ASCENT/GRADIENT 59ft (18m) ▲▲▲   LEVEL OF DIFFICULTY ✛✛✛

PATHS Canal tow path, disused railway track and field paths

LANDSCAPE Open countryside near urban residences

SUGGESTED MAP OS Explorer 219 Wolverhampton & Dudley

START/FINISH Grid reference: SO 870983

DOG FRIENDLINESS Off lead along tow path and disused railway, otherwise under control

PARKING Near Mermaid pub, Wightwick

PUBLIC TOILETS None on route

This is a journey into the 18th and 19th centuries – a time when the canals and railways preceded our modern, noisy road network. The walk follows the tow path of the Staffordshire and Worcestershire Canal and a stretch of disused railway line to Compton. Nearby Wightwick (pronounced 'Wittick') Manor is easy to visit along the route (see While You're There).

CANAL REVOLUTION

If a contest for the Greatest Briton had taken place at the end of the 19th century, one of the main contenders would surely have been James Brindley. He helped to revolutionise Britain's transport system by building a series of remarkable canals that linked virtually all of the major cities in Britain. The Staffordshire and Worcestershire Canal was one of his early constructions, built to link the Severn at Stourport with the Trent at Great Heywood and carry coal from the Staffordshire coalfields. Brindley's waterways were built on the contour principle, following the lie of the land. This approach avoided straight lines of canal, deep cuttings, massive embankments and large groups of lock gates. Work on the Staffordshire and Worcestershire Canal began in 1766 and was eventually completed in 1772. When you walk along the tow path you can imagine the dirty barges of the late 18th and early 19th centuries being hauled along by horses, accompanied by inquisitive children, dogs and local people. Commercial traffic finally ceased on the canal in 1960 and in 1978 the whole waterway, including its buildings and its signs, was designated a conservation area.

As the Industrial Revolution progressed, steam trains effectively replaced canal barges, but there were gaps in the rail network. The Kingswinford branch was built by the Great Western Railway to fill one of these, allowing through traffic from Bridgnorth to Wolverhampton. It opened in 1925 but was never a great success for passengers. It became a freight-only line in 1932, carrying people again briefly during World War II, when it was used to transfer wounded soldiers from the Normandy landings. The last train ran in 1965. The lines were then dismantled and the Kingswinford Railway Walk was introduced to allow local people to use the former line for leisure purposes.

Today pleasure boats use the canal, and its tow path combines with the disused railway to provide a fine urban walk away from the noise of the busy road traffic.

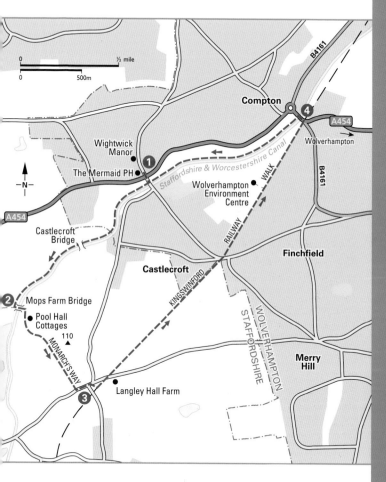

❶ From The Mermaid pub, cross the A454 at the pedestrian crossing to take the lane opposite. Don't cross the bridge, but bear right, descending to the tow path of the Staffordshire and Worcestershire Canal. Turn right (southwest) along the path, and after passing the Cee-Ders Club (on the far side of the canal), you reach open countryside. This stretch of the canal is similar to a river and you are likely to see anglers fishing for perch, roach, chub, bream or carp. Continue beneath bridge No. 55 (Castlecroft Bridge) and along the tow path until you come to bridge No. 54 (Mops Farm Bridge).

❷ Leave the tow path and cross the bridge. Go right past Pool Hall Cottages and follow the waymarkers of the Monarch's Way, heading generally southeast. At first the path is to the right of the field hedge; later it crosses over to the left-hand side until you come to a gap leading out onto Langley Road.

❸ Go left up the road, and immediately past the junction bear right at the postbox, go through a fence gap into the picnic area and descend steps to the dismantled railway. Head left and follow the Kingswinford (South Staffordshire) Railway Walk. This is easy walking and you are likely to meet other walkers and even cyclists. Follow the course of the railway for about 2 miles (3.2km). You will eventually pass beneath the

road bridge near Castlecroft via a kissing gate; following this there are moments when the scene opens up. After passing the Wolverhampton Environment Centre and the remains of Compton Station's platform you come to Compton. Leave the disused railway line and descend to the A454, going left.

❹ Cross the road and then the canal bridge to descend to the tow path. Pass beneath bridge No. 59 and take it back to bridge No. 56, passing a couple of lock gates and a number of moored narrow boats. Go beneath bridge No. 56 and leave the canal, walking onto the pavement of Windmill Lane. Continue towards the main A454 road and cross over to return to The Mermaid in Wightwick.

WHERE TO EAT AND DRINK Eating out in the small front garden of The Mermaid pub watching the world go by is the perfect way to end a perfect day. Children are also welcome. If you visit Wightwick Manor, you can enjoy a quiet leisurely lunch in the Tea Room. Many of the ingredients are grown in the kitchen garden.

● ● ● ●

WHAT TO SEE You may not see a horse-drawn coal barge as you stroll the tow path of the 46-mile (74km) long Staffordshire and Worcestershire Canal, but you are likely to meet a colourful narrowboat making its way through one of the lock gates. Pause a while and watch how it is raised or dropped to another level. Compton Lock, just beyond Compton village, was the first lock to be built on this canal.

● ● ● ●

WHILE YOU'RE THERE Nearby Wightwick Manor was built in 1887 for the Mander family, paint manufacturers from nearby Wolverhampton. The half-timbered house was donated to the National Trust in 1937. The influence of the 19th-century decorative artist William Morris is clear to see. Original Morris wallpapers, Pre-Raphaelite pictures, stained glass by C E Kempe and De Morgan tiles are on display. There are also fine gardens laid out with terraces and pools by Thomas Mawson.

Linking Pedmore and Hagley Park

DISTANCE 4.5 miles (7.2km)	MINIMUM TIME 2hrs

ASCENT/GRADIENT 279ft (85m) ▲▲▲   LEVEL OF DIFFICULTY ✚✚✚

PATHS Field paths, farm tracks and roadside pavement

LANDSCAPE Fields, woods and suburban housing

SUGGESTED MAP OS Explorer 219 Wolverhampton & Dudley

START/FINISH Grid reference: SO 913821

DOG FRIENDLINESS On lead at all times through residential areas, off lead on Wychbury Hill

PARKING Roadside in Pedmore Lane, or Pedmore Hall Lane, Pedmore

PUBLIC TOILETS None on route

For much of this walk there are fine views into Worcestershire over the Clent Hills, and the best of these is from the Obelisk, with Hagley Hall in the valley below. From the suburban West Midlands, town paths take you into the countryside, then link with farm tracks and the North Worcestershire Path, following part of the Monarch's Way over Wychbury Hill.

A STATELY HOUSE

Set below the range of the Clent Hills, on the outskirts of the village of Hagley, is one of the stateliest houses in England. Hagley Hall was the last of the great Palladian houses to be built. It was designed by Sanderson Miller and built between 1754 and 1760 for George, the 1st Lord Lyttelton (who was secretary to the Prince of Wales), on the site of an earlier house. The impressive building is constructed of brown stone, a rich colour that contrasts well with the Clent Hills in the background and the hall's raised lawns. Its roof balustrades, pedimented in pure Classical style, run the length of the four square-towered wings in the tradition of Inigo Jones.

FIRE AND HELLFIRE

In 1925 a serious fire caused a great deal of damage to the interior of the building but, thankfully, it has since been restored to its former glory. The entrance hall is decorated with lovely stucco work and the dining room, one of the rooms most badly affected by the fire, has an impressive rococo ceiling. Rich tapestries and fine Van Dyke paintings are the main feature of the gallery. The 2nd Lord Lyttelton was a founder member of the notorious so-called Hellfire Club of 18th-century aristocratic libertines, along with Sir Francis Dashwood of West Wycombe. Littleton was a great gambler and on one occasion gambled the whole of Hagley Hall against a single painting. Luckily he won the bet and kept his home.

Over the centuries Hagley Hall has entertained many important visitors – great poets, the country's top architects, scientists and politicians, including Prime Minister William Gladstone. The hall is set in some 350 acres (142ha) of imaginatively landscaped deer park, with an Ionic temple, a weathered rotunda and a folly in the form of a Gothic ruin. The Obelisk was built in 1758. Behind, the Clent Hills rise to 997ft (304m), forming the perfect backdrop for the views that will follow you along this walk.

Today Hagley is home to Lord and Lady Cobham and is now well established as a premier location for conferences, business meetings, product launches, fairy-tale weddings and dinner parties. It can also be visited on a guided tour.

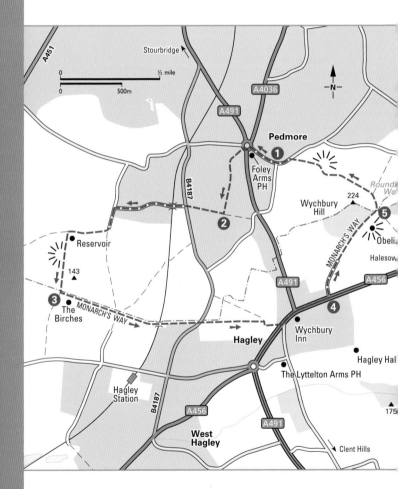

❶ From Pedmore Lane walk into the centre of Pedmore to a roundabout junction with the A491. Go around the island, cross the A491 and continue down the public bridleway signed 'Hagley Road Nos. 280, 280A, 280B, 280C and 280D'. Follow this path along the back of houses and past a primary school then more houses, bearing right at a path junction.

2 At the footpath T-junction, go right and continue on footpaths to the B4187 (Worcester Lane). Cross the lane and the main line railway bridge into Quarry Park Road. Continue along the path, following the public bridleway sign to Ounty John Lane, eventually turning left onto a stone track until you come to open countryside. When you reach the track junction go right, soon passing a Severn Trent reservoir. At the end of the reservoir, go immediately left and walk along a farm track over undulating ground, with views to the right towards the hills and Bewdley.

3 At the junction of paths by The Birches copse, go left (east) over a stile along the North Worcestershire Path, Monarch's Way. Initially this is to the left of The Birches, then it veers to the other side of a field hedge, via a stile, descending to cross the railway line once again. It then continues straight ahead through a small housing estate in Hagley, first along the road and then on a footpath beyond No. 60. Eventually the Way comes to a road corner on the B4187 (Worcester Lane). Cross the road, following the footpath sign opposite, and take the hedged path via a stile and continue ahead at the bottom of a series of fields, crossing two stiles, until you reach the busy A456. Go left beside the road, walking to the left of the traffic island and cross the A491 (Stourbridge Road).

4 After following the pavement along the A456 for about 350yds (320m), go left up Monument Lane. Take the lane to the end, then continue on the Monarch's Way via two gates as it climbs towards the Obelisk on Wychbury Hill. Beyond a stile the path goes to the left of the monument and along the side of Roundhill Wood to a junction of footpaths by the trees.

5 Take the path on the left through a kissing gate and a belt of trees and, through a gate, continue down a fenced path, turning right to return to Pedmore Lane.

WHERE TO EAT AND DRINK There are three pubs in the vicinity. The Foley Arms in Pedmore is at the start and finish of the walk and offers decent food. The Wychbury Inn specialises in Thai cuisine, and The Lyttelton Arms, close to Hagley Hall, is more of a 'gastro-pub'.

••••

WHAT TO SEE Back in the 18th century Hagley Hall was praised for its fine gardens. Then, in the 19th century, the Kidderminster–Birmingham road (the A456) was built, cutting off Wychbury Hill from the main garden, leaving the garden ornaments of the Obelisk and the Temple of Theseus on the wrong side of the road.

••••

WHILE YOU'RE THERE Give way to the temptation of the Clent Hills and visit the country park (National Trust), which covers some 425 acres (172ha), to the south of this walk. Much of the area is covered with deciduous woodland, gorse and heather. Stroll up to Adam's Hill and the Four Stones for with a view that embraces the Shropshire, Abberley, Malvern and Welsh hills.

Overleaf: Wychbury Hill from The Birches (Walk 2)

Dallying in Dudley

DISTANCE 3.5 miles (5.7km)	MINIMUM TIME 2hrs

ASCENT/GRADIENT 328ft (100m) ▲▲▲   LEVEL OF DIFFICULTY ✦✦✦

PATHS Parkland paths and roadside pavements

LANDSCAPE Nature reserve and streets around Dudley

SUGGESTED MAP OS Explorer 219 Wolverhampton & Dudley

START/FINISH Grid reference: SO 949907

DOG FRIENDLINESS Off lead in park, otherwise under control

PARKING Dudley Zoo pay car park, Castle Hill, Dudley

PUBLIC TOILETS In Dudley

The Black Country originally took its name from the dark, coal-stained soil which characterises this corner of the county where the old boundaries of Worcestershire, Shropshire, Staffordshire and Warwickshire meet. But for many it truly earned the name in the 18th and 19th centuries, when the Industrial Revolution took off. The mines, factories and furnaces belched out their blackening soot, so the sky was 'black by day and red by night'. This walk offers the opportunity to explore the unique history of Dudley and the surrounding countryside, including the Wren's Nest National Nature Reserve.

INDUSTRIAL DUDLEY

You could be forgiven for expecting the capital of the Black Country to be an old industrial town with little to offer the visitor, but Dudley is a large, vibrant place with a fascinating history that reveals an amazing contrast of English heritage. From Saxon times up to the Civil War the town developed much like any other in Britain. In the Middle Ages it became a country market town, with a town hall and small shops dotted around its central market place. The arrival of coal-mining and iron-working in the 17th century brought massive changes to the area and Dudley steadily expanded to become the main business centre of the Black Country.

It was here in the 1620s that Dud Dudley first experimented with using coal (as coke) for smelting iron. Another Dudley man, Abraham Darby, at Coalbrookdale, developed the process and the town's later ironworks dominated the area until the middle of the 20th century. The Black Country Living Museum reveals how tough life would have been during the early days of the Industrial Revolution. In the late 18th century the Stourbridge and Dudley Canal was built to link with the Staffordshire and Worcestershire Canal to the west and the rest of the Birmingham canal system.

Dudley No. 1 Canal joins the Stourbridge Canal at the bottom of the Delphi Locks. Today mining activities are a thing of the past and Dudley is a clean place to live and visit. The 1817 Regency Gothic Church of St Thomas the Apostle, with its towering spire, dominates the town's skyline. A number of other attractive old buildings remain, including the landmark Crown Inn, with its unusual bartizan (corner turret with windows), and Baylies's Charity, a charity school built in 1820 which features two appealing statues of schoolboys dressed in the uniform of the day.

The Wren's Nest National Nature Reserve, Britain's first National Nature Reserve for Geology, is famous for its fossils, the best-known being a trilobite christened the 'Dudley Bug' or the 'Dudley Locust'. It forms the centrepiece of the town's coat of arms.

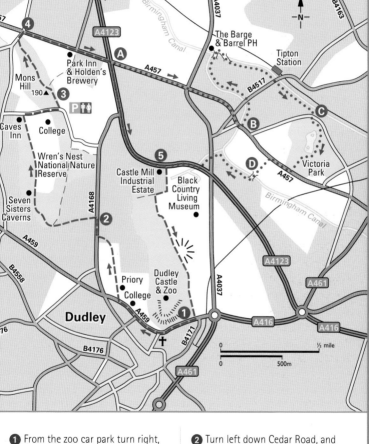

1 From the zoo car park turn right, up Castle Hill, past the zoo's visitor entrance. Bear right, along Broadway, down past the college. You'll soon reach the 12th-century priory ruins in Priory Park. Go right and wander through to the far end of the park, then go left down Woodland Avenue, bearing right and crossing over the A4168 (Priory Road).

2 Turn left down Cedar Road, and continue past a school to enter the southern part of Wren's Nest National Nature Reserve via a stile, by an information board. Continue ahead for 100yds (91m), turn left up the long flight of steps and continue along the higher footpath, first left and then right. This path leads near to the Seven Sisters Caverns. Continue ahead and you will eventually emerge between the Caves Inn and the college grounds. You are now on Wrens Hill Road near the inn. Go right along the road and just past the college buildings to a stile on the left.

3 Cross the stile and follow the path that takes you over craggy Mons Hill. Eventually, where the path divides, take the left fork, initially down steps, until you near some houses. Reaching Parkes Hall Road, turn right along the road until you come to the A457 (Sedgley Road West).

4 Turn right and follow the A457 for about 750yds (686m), then go right along the A4123 (Birmingham New Road). After 0.25 miles (400m) of easy walking, the road arcs left,

and beyond a bus stop look out for the Castle Mill industrial estate on the right.

5 A few paces up the Castle Hill industrial estate access, go left through a scruffy barrier onto a footpath, then continue along the Limekiln Walk path through the woodland by Castle Hill. There are many paths through this woodland, but try to keep to the left-hand paths going southwards near to the edge of the trees for over 0.5 miles (800m). This is pleasant walking and soon the path reaches the open where it becomes a track and passes to the left of the Dudley Zoo enclosures, with a view over the Black Country Living Museum. Continue through to the zoo car park.

WHERE TO EAT AND DRINK A local favourite is the Caves Inn, where children and dogs are allowed in the games room. Light refreshments are offered at the Black Country Living Museum and Dudley Castle. The Barge and Barrel at nearby Tipton is a delightful canalside pub where you can enjoy the narrowboat world. Real ale fans will enjoy The Park Inn, the brewery tap for the adjacent Holden's Brewery.

● ● ● ●

WHAT TO SEE Keep your eye open for fossils when you visit the Wren's Nest National Nature Reserve. Around 425 million years ago this area was submerged, forming part of the Silurian Sea, and a wide range of sea creatures including trilobites and brachiopods inhabited the coral reefs. Today the site has been stripped largely of its fossils – collecting is discouraged and hammers are definitely not allowed. However, there are lime kilns to see, and children will enjoy exploring the Seven Sisters Caverns and Cherry Hole.

● ● ● ●

WHILE YOU'RE THERE Visit the Black Country Living Museum, which lies in the shadow of Dudley Castle. The museum is a reconstructed canalside village with a pub, shops, chapel, ironworks, miner's experience and boat trips from the wharf into the Dudley Tunnel, with its caverns and basins. Dudley Zoo, in the grounds of Dudley Castle, is also a magnet for children of all ages. There are seals in the moat, llamas roaming the slopes below the keep, and a tropical rain forest and Adventure Land.

Along the Birmingham Canal

DISTANCE 7 miles (11.3km)   MINIMUM TIME 2hrs 45min

ASCENT/GRADIENT 328ft (100m) ▲▲▲   LEVEL OF DIFFICULTY ✦✦✦

SEE MAP AND INFORMATION PANEL FOR WALK 3

Follow Walk 3 as far as the A4123 junction (Point **Ⓐ**), cross it and then the A4037, then continue along the A457, which becomes Sedgley Road West. Just after crossing the B4517 (Owen Street), cross the canal and turn left to go down to the tow path of the Birmingham Canal. Soon pass close to The Fountain pub (Point **Ⓑ**).

Continue along the right bank of the canal. When you get close to The Barge and Barrel pub, cross the footbridge to the left bank and go right to pass by Factory Locks. The tow path then crosses back to the right bank, via the Wood Street Footbridge. After passing by Tipton Railway Station the route goes beneath the B4517 road bridge. Leave the canal at the next road bridge, beyond a boatyard, and go right into Watery Lane. Cross over Queen's Road into Victoria Park (Point **Ⓒ**). Walk through the park, passing the ponds and various play areas, to emerge at the top, on Park Lane West (the A457). Turn right for 100yds (93m), then left at the crossing, into Baker Street. At the end of the street cross the footbridge to descend back onto the tow path of the Birmingham Canal (Point **Ⓓ**).

The Birmingham Canal once carried the products of industrial Britain around the Midlands and across the country. It is part of a network of canals that makes you realise just how inventive our predecessors were. Today the canal is a leisure facility and you will see narrowboats negotiating their way up the canal in the summer.

Go right along the tow path through a gate, then bear left to go beneath the A4037, the Dudley Road Bridge, and A4123, the Birmingham New Road Bridge, which bring you near the tunnel at the rear 'Narrowboat' entrance – a direct canal link to the Black Country Living Museum. Take the opportunity to visit this fascinating outdoor attraction. Built to preserve the industrial heritage of the area, it offers an intriguing view of the Black Country as it was. Historic buildings from around the area have been rebuilt to re-create the Heart of Industrial Britain. A trip down the coal mine is a real educational experience.

Climb steps up to the A4123 and go left until you come to Castle Mill industrial estate, a road to the left. Here rejoin Walk 3 at Point **❺**.

A Walk in The Leasowes

DISTANCE 4 miles (6.4km)	**MINIMUM TIME** 1hr 30min

ASCENT/GRADIENT 394ft (120m) ▲▲▲   **LEVEL OF DIFFICULTY** +++

PATHS Pavements, field paths and tow path

LANDSCAPE Nature reserve and open countryside around urban area

SUGGESTED MAP OS Explorer 219 Wolverhampton & Dudley

START/FINISH Grid reference: SO 975839

DOG FRIENDLINESS Off lead along tow path, otherwise under control

PARKING The Leasowes car park, off A458

PUBLIC TOILETS None on route

The Leasowes was a mixed farm of arable and pasture when William Shenstone (1714–63) inherited it from his uncle in the early 1740s. William freely admitted he would rather be known as a poet than as a farmer, and he set about transforming the surrounding fields into a *ferme ornée* – an ornamental farm, or the Romantic movement's answer to landscape gardening. Shenstone was not a rich landowner, however, so many of the innovations he made were borne of necessity rather than extravagance. He transformed the local water courses into cascades and pools, planted trees and installed benches and even strategically sited 'ruins' to enhance the pleasurable aspect.

In 1755 a collection of his poems became a bestseller, and Shenstone could relax into the role of garden innovator. It wasn't until after his death, however, that *A Description of The Leasowes* was published by Robert Dodsley, and the landscape's fame spread far and wide, attracting salubrious visitors such as Benjamin Franklin, Thomas Jefferson and even John Wesley.

A LANDSCAPE OVERTAKEN

The arrival of the Dudley No. 2 canal in 1779 finally interrupted the sylvan scene, and from then on Shenstone's vision began to fade. The parklands came into municipal ownership in 1932, and the Ruined Priory survived until demolition in the 1960s, but it had to wait until 2008 for the centre piece, Virgil's Grove, to be restored with the aid of a Heritage Lottery Fund grant.

Today The Leasowes is recognised as an important milestone in landscape design, with English Heritage listing and a management plan to ensure this important parkland is retained for future generations.

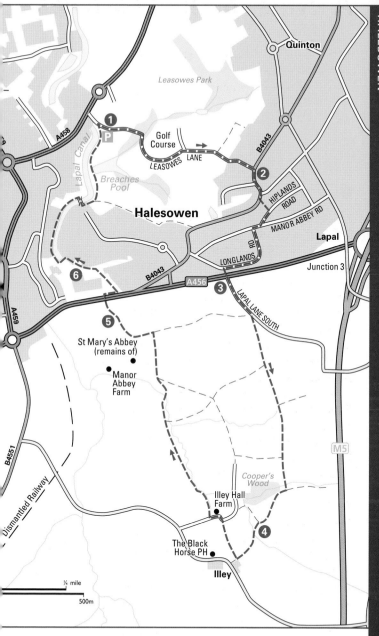

① Leave the car park at the north end by walking past the Warden's base, uphill along a tarmac driveway. At the junction, near houses, bear right through a gateway and continue along the driveway past a pool, then between the greens below Halesowen

Golf Club clubhouse. Where the tarmac track arcs left near the clubhouse, turn right. At the top the drive leads into Leasowes Lane.

② At the end of the lane go right along Manor Lane (B4043). After passing Stennels Avenue, the lane bends sharp right. Here go left up a narrow public footpath to the right of No. 61. Follow this fenced footpath into Hiplands Road; go right, then right again into Manor Abbey Road at the T-junction. In 20yds (18m), go left down Longlands Road and continue as it bends right. After passing Lavina and Christopher roads, go left through a footpath barrier to reach the A456.

3 Cross the road at the pedestrian crossing and go down Lapal Lane South opposite. After 275yds (251m), go right over a stile and into open countryside. Follow the direction of the fingerpost signed to Illey, and take the path up along the left edge of a field. Go left over a second stile and bear right to the hedged path, heading south. Where another path joins from the left, the path becomes a track. At a junction of paths, continue ahead, then go through trees to the left of Cooper's Wood. At the end of this, over a stile, go right. Cross another stile, then bear quarter left to a stile to cross pasture. Over a stile the path arcs right, and then left over another stile onto a track.

4 Follow this track and in 100yds (91m) go right over a pair of stiles. (If you walk to the end of the track you reach a road, with The Black Horse on the corner opposite.) Continue to the right of a field hedge, with a football pitch on the other side. At the field corner, go left over a stile and walk around the bottom end of the football field, leaving via the football club gate onto the farm drive near Illey Hall Farm. Go left along the drive for 30yds (27m), then right over a stile and take the path to the left of the field hedge. Follow this path, soon merging with the Monarch's Way, over several fields and stiles, later crossing to the other side of the hedge via a stile where there is a stream to the right. The path arcs right to a bridge and becomes a farm track arcing left towards Manor Abbey Farm. Bear right as you approach the farm, picking out a field corner stile and continuing across a large cultivated field.

5 Cross the stile and go left, then bear right over a footbridge to a pair of stiles that take you back to the side of the A456. Go right for 25yds (23m), then cross at the crossing. Go right, then left to follow the footpath signed 'Leasowes Park and Breaches Pool'.

6 This path passes along the back of residential properties. Continue ahead to the right of a chain-link fence and soon the path becomes the tow path of the Lapal Canal (formally known as the Dudley No. 2). The canal is overgrown, and there are houses up to the right. After 400yds (366m) a bank crosses the canal, just before a former lock. Cross this and head along the tow path, now to the right of the canal (water visible here), with The Leasowes to your right. In 150yds (137m) enjoy the fine view over Breaches Pool, then continue up the tow path and return to the car park.

WHERE TO EAT AND DRINK A local favourite with walkers is the Black Horse pub at Illey. The food is standard pub fare, but there are usually some special offers and the Sunday roasts are popular.

Around Woodgate Valley Country Park

DISTANCE 3.5 miles (5.7km)   MINIMUM TIME 1hr 30min

ASCENT/GRADIENT 49ft (15m) ▲▲▲   LEVEL OF DIFFICULTY ✦✦✦

PATHS Grassy footpaths and tracks

LANDSCAPE Country park

SUGGESTED MAP OS Explorers 219 Wolverhampton & Dudley; 220 Birmingham

START/FINISH Grid reference: SO 994829

DOG FRIENDLINESS Off lead around park

PARKING Woodgate Valley Country Park

PUBLIC TOILETS Country Park visitor centre building

Birmingham is surrounded by country parks, which act as the lungs of the city. Woodgate Valley Country Park is one of these vital green spaces and this walk takes you past an urban farm complex and along the side of the babbling Bourn Brook, which runs the length of the valley to the River Rea at Cannon Hill Park.

WOODGATE VALLEY COUNTRY PARK

The park comprises some 450 acres (182ha) of meadows, hedgerows and woodland on the western edge of Birmingham. It was originally a mixture of farms and smallholdings and every effort has been made to retain its rural appeal. Threatened by development, it was designated a Country Park in 1984. A programme of hedge and tree replanting has taken place, and the visitor centre opened in 1987.

The woodland, ponds and meadows have now become home to a vast range of wildlife and hundreds of species of plants and flowers. The meadowlands near the start of this walk, known as Pinewoods, are a treat to stroll through on a warm summer's day. Pheasants, kingfishers, cuckoos, chiffchaffs, whitethroats and willow warblers are regular visitors, and if you're lucky you may see a long-eared owl or even a marsh harrier. Butterflies are also favourite summer visitors.

During 2001, the foot and mouth epidemic resulted in the closure of many footpaths in the Midlands countryside and Woodgate Valley Park became a refuge for walkers and ramblers from outlying areas. Although it is close to so many urban roads, you can still enjoy peace and tranquillity away from the noise of traffic. Houses surround it, yet very few can be seen when you are walking the footpaths along the side of Bourn Brook.

UNDERGROUND CANAL

Beneath the parkland are the remains of part of the Lapal Tunnel on the Dudley No. 2 Canal, which connected Halesowen with Selly

Oak. It is one of the longest canal tunnels in England and a reminder that the industrial side of Birmingham is never too far away, even if you can't actually see it.

The canal was built in 1790 despite fierce local opposition as industrial expansion in the West Midlands was proceeding at a frightening pace. Measuring only 9ft (2.7m) wide and 9ft (2.7m) from water level to ceiling, it gradually fell into disuse with competition from the railways. Following mining subsidence in 1917, the tunnel was closed and finally sealed off in 1926, though there is an active campaign to reopen it some time in the future.

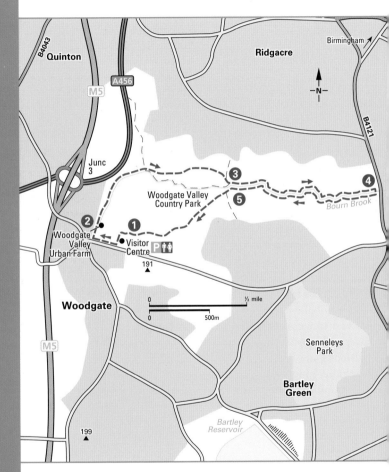

1 From the bottom of the visitor centre car park, turn left on the main road, and then right on the pavement, down the hill for 100yds (93m), bearing right at the roundabout. Turn right along Woodgate Lane for 20yds (18m), then right again down Watery Lane, signposted to Bourn Brook, Harbourne and Selly Oak.

2 When you reach the farm access gate, bear left along the tarmac footpath by the side of a stream – the Bourn Brook – with the bridleway up to the left. This path arcs right, passing two footbridges over the brook. At the second footbridge, do not cross it but bear left past the large oak tree and a bench seat and walk along a footpath that arcs away from the stream towards an area of young trees. In about 100yds (93m), bear right and in a few more paces right again, beyond a white-tipped marker post. The path dips back into the woods briefly before emerging in an open area. Follow the grassy ride down the left-hand side of the clearing. At a junction of paths, by a bench, take the right-hand option, crossing the meadow.

❸ Another footpath comes in from the left, and you then reach another junction of footpaths at which you continue ahead. Soon another path merges from the left and you bear right towards a rather high footbridge over the stream. Do not cross it; instead bear left and follow the footpath on the left side of Bourn Brook. This leads into the trees and there follows a very pleasant stroll through the park, always close to the bank of the stream (ignore a subsequent footbridge).

❹ All too soon you will hear the noise of traffic on the B4121 ahead. Just before you reach the road, go right over the footbridge and follow the footpath down the other side of the stream. The path passes close to housing, but this is barely visible and the country feel is maintained until you reach the high footbridge once again.

❺ Do not go over the footbridge, but leave the Bourn Brook behind and bear half left to take a grassy footpath that crosses open land diagonally with houses to your left (do not go left towards the houses). Through a tree belt maintain your direction over a second open area, diverging away from the houses. At the end, cross the footbridge in the far corner and bear right to follow the path near the field-edge, firstly in woods, then passing by a football pitch to arrive back at the visitor centre.

WHERE TO EAT AND DRINK Woodgate Valley Café, in the visitor centre, is a popular eating place for walkers, offering sandwiches, toasties, jacket potatoes, curries and Cornish pasties. There are picnic tables and benches in the park area where children and dogs are always welcome. The Old Crown is in Carter's Lane if you would prefer a pint, but children and dogs are not admitted.

● ● ● ●

WHAT TO SEE Despite its urban surroundings, there are several remnants of the old rural landscape still visible. Hole Farm's former farmhouse now houses the pony trekking centre, and the nearby Watery Lane was once a route for salt carriers, crossing the country from Lincolnshire to Wales. The hedgerows here can trace their origins to the 13th century. The ancient lane encountered towards the end of the walk was once the main thoroughfare in the area, and maybe over 500 years old.

● ● ● ●

WHILE YOU'RE THERE Take time to visit the rare and unusual breeds of farm animals at the Woodgate Valley Urban Farm, who live alongside more familiar domestic breeds and pets. The farm is a registered charity, and maintained by volunteers from the local community.

Discovering Sandwell Valley Country Park

DISTANCE 4.5 miles (7.2km)	MINIMUM TIME 2hrs

ASCENT/GRADIENT 66ft (20m) ▲▲▲   LEVEL OF DIFFICULTY ✦✦✦

PATHS Lakeside paths and tracks

LANDSCAPE Country park with many lakes

SUGGESTED MAP OS Explorer 220 Birmingham

START/FINISH Grid reference: SP 035927

DOG FRIENDLINESS Off lead in park

PARKING RSPB visitor centre

PUBLIC TOILETS For visitors to Sandwell Park Farm; otherwise none on route

Once upon a time there was a 12th-century Benedictine monastery on the site of an earlier hermitage in the area now called Sandwell Valley Country Park, situated at the northeastern edge of West Bromwich. The monastery was closed down in 1525 on the directions of Cardinal Wolsey, then in 1705 Sandwell Hall was erected on the site for the Earl of Dartmouth, incorporating some of the old priory buildings. The hall was demolished in 1928 with the development of Hamstead Colliery, which came to dominate the whole area. When the pit was nationalised in the 1940s it was one of the largest in South Staffordshire, outside Cannock Chase, with nearly 1,000 men working underground here and at the nearby Sandwell Park Colliery.

FROM COLLIERY TO COUNTRY PARK

The collieries closed in the early 1960s, since when the land has been transformed into an urban oasis. The earthworks and spoil from the site became a series of artificial lakes, landscaped to produce an amazingly different scene. Sandwell Valley Country Park is now a fascinating area of lakes and 2,000 acres (810ha) of parkland developed from the old colliery sites and the remains of the Sandwell Hall Estate. The park has become a major leisure facility, with three golf courses, walking routes, a Millennium Cycle Route and two off-road cycle paths, which have been specially designed for mountain bikes. Around 20,000 people visit the park each year. Wildfowl flock to the area in large numbers and the Royal Society for the Protection of Birds (RSPB) has established a nature reserve nearby, which covers some 25 acres (10ha) of the reclaimed Hamstead Colliery site.

VICTORIAN FARM

Forge Mill visitor centre can be found on the other side of Forge Lane, and Swan Pool leads to footbridges over the noisy

M5 motorway. Sandwell Park Farm was also part of the Earl of Dartmouth's estate and was extensively restored in 1981 to show the traditional Victorian methods of farming. The farm has a walled kitchen garden, craft shops, a rare breeds area and a heritage centre where you can see the findings of a 1980s archaeological dig at Sandwell Priory.

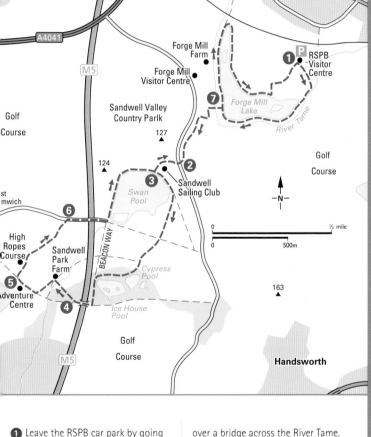

1 Leave the RSPB car park by going left of the visitor centre building onto a footpath. This leads down to a path along the dike crest between the River Tame and Forge Mill Lake. Continue along this footpath which arcs gently right and look out for the many birds on the lake, as well as Canada geese and ducks on the river. As you work your way around the lake you will come to a gateway where you go left over a bridge across the River Tame. Turn immediately left to continue on a tarmac path/cycleway that leads down to Forge Lane.

2 Cross the busy lane with great care, and walk to the right of the Sandwell Valley Sailing Club premises (in former pithead buildings), then bear left until you come to the shore of Swan Pool.

❸ Here turn left and stroll around the side of the pool for 150yds (137m), then bear left again on a footpath, via a kissing that leads across meadowland away from the water's edge, initially alongside the Pool's fence. Through a kissing gate, cross the track and continue ahead on a hedged footpath heading generally southwest. At a junction of paths go left through a barrier and proceed through the trees, then go right to follow the narrow path to the north bank of both Cypress and Ice House pools. Continue ahead to leave the lakes and emerge on a concrete lane by the side of the noisy M5. (If you had continued ahead at the junction of paths instead of going left, you would have arrived at the same position.) Go left and stroll along this wide lane. At a junction, bear right and take the footbridge to cross over the M5.

❹ Across the bridge go right down steps, now on the Beacon Way, and wind amid trees on the path up to Sandwell Park Farm, where there are toilet facilities and you can get light refreshments.

❺ Leave the farm through the car park and continue along the lane, turning right opposite the Adventure Centre through a kissing gate. Walk ahead along the signed public footpath heading northeastwards within a belt of trees. (To the left you will see the high ropes course.) When you reach the end of the hedged area, bear left and proceed along a tarmac path towards the motorway, until you reach a junction.

❻ Go right here along Salters Lane and return over the M5, via a second footbridge. Take the tarmac path that goes to the left of Swan Pool and continue left past the sailing cub premises to busy Forge Lane. Cross the lane and take the footpath back to the bridge over the River Tame to reach the junction of footpaths by the edge of Forge Mill Lake.

❼ Go left and walk around the lake, leaving the River Tame and going right just before the railway bridge. Keep close to the lake shore until turning left at a sign – this path takes you back to the visitor centre at the start of the walk.

WHERE TO EAT AND DRINK Children are welcomed in the tea rooms of Sandwell Park Farm (entry fee), but not dogs. A Sandwell Valley full English breakfast will sustain even the hungriest walker and is available until 2.30pm every day, or perhaps you would prefer a jacket potato, pasty, pie or a salad. To quench your thirst you could visit one of the many pubs in West Bromwich, a historic town pleasantly updated, 3 miles (4.8km) west.

●●●●

WHAT TO SEE The RSPB reserve in Sandwell Valley Country Park is an important West Midlands home to a wide variety of birds and attracts around 150 species each year. Volunteers often staff the various viewing hides. Highlights in the reserve may include goosander and snipe in winter, lapwings and little ringed plover in spring and whitethroats through the summer. Look out too for a hobby, hunting for larger insects around the pool edges.

Hay Head Wood and the Walsall Waterfront

DISTANCE 3.75 miles (6km)	MINIMUM TIME 1hr 15min

ASCENT/GRADIENT 66ft (20m) ▲▲▲   LEVEL OF DIFFICULTY ✦✦✦

PATHS Field paths and tow paths

LANDSCAPE Canalside and urban parkland

SUGGESTED MAP OS Explorer 220 Birmingham

START/FINISH Grid reference: SP 041990

DOG FRIENDLINESS Off lead along tow path, otherwise under control

PARKING Hay Head Wood Nature Reserve car park

PUBLIC TOILETS None on route

The walk starts from the Hay Head Wood Nature Reserve and proceeds along the tow path of the Rushall Canal, where once horses pulled heavily laden narrow boats of limestone to flux mills and cement factories in the Black Country.

As you explore the history of the Black Country, it becomes clear that Walsall was very much at the hub of the Industrial Revolution in 19th-century Britain. Each large town in the area had its role to play, and limestone, used as flux in the iron foundries and for cement production in the construction of canal buildings, was mined in the countryside around Walsall. The town also became England's centre for the manufacture of leather goods and fine saddlery – the nickname of the local football team is the Saddlers. Much of old Walsall has disappeared, but it has become a vibrant modern town, surrounded by numerous parks, which offer a link with its industrial past.

THE 'CURLY WYRLEY' AND THE RUSHALL

John Wilkinson, a famous pioneering 'ironmaster' opened up Hay Head Wood for limestone excavation in the 18th century. The rock was transported along two canals – the Wyrley and Essington, and the Rushall. The Wyrley and Essington was completed in 1797, with nine locks designed to lift the lime-laden barges some 65ft (20m) up to the Longwood Junction near Aldridge. This contour canal, affectionately known as the Curly Wyrley, follows the lie of the land and winds its way from Hay Head Park up to Lime Pits Farm and Park Lime Pits Local Nature Reserve, then on to the north of Birmingham. The Rushall Canal was built as a 2.5-mile (4km) connection between the Wyrley and Essington Canal and the Tame Valley Canal. Limestone extraction finally ceased in the 1920s, but remnants of the canal wharf buildings, pit shafts and pump housings can still be seen. The land around the lime pits has since been reclaimed by nature.

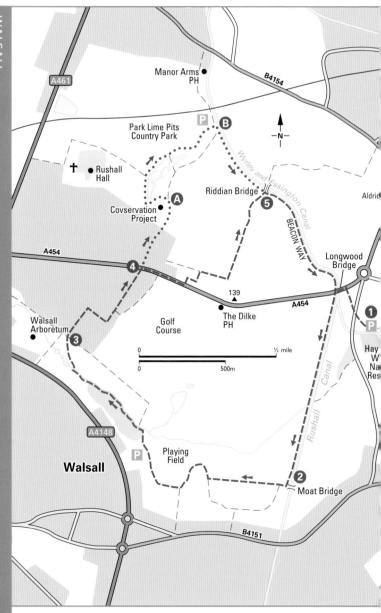

A461

Park Lime Pits
Country Park

P B

←N→

Wyrley and Essington Canal

✝ ● Rushall
Hall

A Riddian Bridge 5

Covservation ●
Project

Aldrid

BEACON WAY

A454

4 Longwood
Bridge

Walsall
Arboretum
●
3

139
▲
● The Dilke
PH

A454

Golf
Course

0   ½ mile
0   500m

Rushall Canal

1
P

Hay
W
Na
Res

A4148

P Playing
Field

Walsall

2
Moat Bridge

B4151

● From the car park proceed over Longwood Lane, now on the Beacon Way, through a lay-by and on to the Longwood Bridge. Cross it to descend left to the tow path of the Rushall Canal. Go right (southwest) and walk past the canal junction, now off the Beacon Way, along the side of the very straight part of the canal.

● After 1,100yds (1km) you will come to Moat Bridge(do not cross). Go right along the hedged track. Shortly a gravel track leads left. Follow this briefly but maintain your direction from the canal along the edge of a field and through little copses of trees, eventually to skirt the edge of a cricket pitch. The path arcs left to the end of King George Avenue. Keep ahead past another cricket pitch before swinging right to a municipal depot and parking area. Cross the car park, heading for an exit on the opposite side by a dog waste bin. Join a tarmac path, now to the left side of a stream. After about 700yds (640m), turn right over a stone footbridge, and then left along the right-hand side of a children's play area up to reach a tarmac footway.

3 Head right up the footway to leave the park area, then cross over Buchanan Road and continue up the footpath until you reach Argyle Road. Turn right and follow the road as it arcs round to the left. Now turn right on Fernleigh Road and follow this to the main A454.

4 Cross over the A454 and turn right, soon joining the grass verge. In around 250yds (229m) go left over a stile by a footpath sign to Riddian Bridge. The path goes off to the right of a farm building, then dog-legs left to reach a hedge line on the far side of the field. Finger posts give the rough direction, eventually on a faint path through vegetation to reach Riddian Bridge.

5 Descend to the tow path of the Wyrley and Essington Canal and turn right. This is easy walking, with just a few ducks and perhaps a heron or two for company. You may see fishermen on the banks of the canal attempting to catch some of the roach, tench, carp and pike that live in the waters. In about 0.5 miles (800m) you come to Longwood Bridge. Beyond the bridge, exit with the Beacon Way signs to the A454. Cross the canal and bear right to return to the car park at the nature reserve.

WHERE TO EAT AND DRINK The Manor Arms, near Park Lime Pits Country Park, is a traditional canalside pub serving food and real ale. Children and dogs are made very welcome, and Sunday lunch is a special treat. Alternatively, you could try The Dilke pub along the A454 (Aldridge Road) or one of the many pubs, restaurants and eateries in Walsall itself.

● ● ● ●

WHAT TO SEE The area around Park Lime Pits Local Nature Reserve has become a haven for wildlife. More than 100 bird species have been recorded here. Moorhens, coots, mallards and grebes can be seen around the clear pools near the reed beds, while bullfinches and buntings inhabit the stubble fields, which are specially managed to encourage wildlife. Although industrial in origin, the site has actually changed very little since the last pits were worked more than 170 years ago. The water quality in the deep pools is so good that freshwater crayfish, endangered elsewhere in the country, flourish here.

● ● ● ●

WHILE YOU'RE THERE The Walsall Arboretum, off the corner of Lichfield Street and Broadway North, was formed in 1874 by the Walsall Arboretum and Lake Company. They rented 7 acres (2.8ha) of land from the landowners, Lord Hatherton and Sir George Mellish, to provide a facility for croquet, archery and quoits, with two lakes for angling and boating.

Park Lime Pits

DISTANCE 4.75 miles (7.7km)   MINIMUM TIME 1hr 45min

ASCENT/GRADIENT 66ft (20m) ▲▲▲   LEVEL OF DIFFICULTY +++

SEE MAP AND INFORMATION PANEL FOR WALK 8

After crossing the A454 at Point ➍, go left along the pavement of Mellish Road up to Mellish Drive. Turn right and walk to the end of Mellish Drive, crossing Stencills Road to a kissing gate. Continue into open countryside on the footpath. If you come in autumn, you will pass between designated stubble fields where the stubble is left after the harvest to provide a suitable environment for local birdlife – yellowhammers, reed buntings and a variety of finches feed on the leftover grain. The farmer is pioneering a conservation project leaving strips of land free from pesticides and fertilisers in order to encourage wildlife back to his 57 acres (23ha) of grass, wheat and barley fields. As you walk along, notice the abundance of wild flowers growing around the field-edges.

When you reach a waymarked junction of footpaths, bear left through the fence gap into the trees of Park Lime Pits Local Nature Reserve (Point ➊). Follow the footpath to the main pool where you go left up steps to follow the path along the pool edge. You may pass people fishing for the large carp and pike that frequent the pool. From 1417 to the mid-19th century limestone was burnt here to make lime, and this was dispatched across Britain via the Rushall Canal and the wider canal system. Following the demise of the lime industry, the pits were closed in 1865 and planted with trees. Today they have been flooded to make an attractive leisure place for local people.

At the far end of the pool descend steps and bear left up further steps to progress into the open, looking southwest to see Rushall Hall and St Michael's Church. The hall was mentioned as the Manor in the Domesday Book but was dismantled after the Civil War. It was rebuilt in 1846. James Cranston built St Michael's Church in 1856 and its fine spire was added in 1867. Take the left fork and continue northeastwards alongside a well laid hedge until you reach Lime Pits car park via a kissing gate by the side of the Wyrley and Essington Canal (Point ➋).

At the canal, turn right and walk along the tow path. This is easy walking along a contour canal, with pleasant views all around. You may see cattle in the fields opposite drinking from the canal. At Riddian Bridge, rejoin the route of Walk 8 at Point ➎.

Discover Birmingham's Jewellery Quarter

DISTANCE 4 miles (6.4km)   MINIMUM TIME 1hr 45min

ASCENT/GRADIENT 16ft (5m) ▲▲▲   LEVEL OF DIFFICULTY +++

PATHS Tow paths and street pavements

LANDSCAPE City centre buildings, factories and canals

SUGGESTED MAP OS Explorer 220 Birmingham, or AA Street by Street: Birmingham, Wolverhampton

START/FINISH Grid reference: SP 064877

DOG FRIENDLINESS On lead at all times

PARKING Northwood Street pay-and-display car park

PUBLIC TOILETS Vyse Street

Birmingham's growth in the Industrial Revolution was vast and overwhelming. The quiet country town of the 16th century had been subsumed by one of the world's first manufacturing cities by the middle of the 18th century, though it wasn't until 1889 that Queen Victoria recognised its city status with a royal charter.

A HALLMARK'S ORIGIN

Foremost amongst those who created this industrial powerhouse was Matthew Boulton (1728–1809), whose partnership with Scottish engineer James Watt (1736–1819) developed a pioneering steam engine. Boulton was first and foremost a manufacturer, with a speciality in buttons and buckles. From his huge Soho Manufactory on the north side of the town he expanded into coins, silver plate and other items.

Boulton's enterprise was hampered by its distance from the nearest Assay Office in Chester. Goods were lost, damaged, copied or stolen on the journey between Birmingham and Cheshire. Teaming up with the cutlers of Sheffield, Boulton petitioned in London for new local offices. Whilst there, he stayed in The Crown and Anchor Tavern on the Strand. When Sheffield and Birmingham received their new Assay Offices by an Act of Parliament in 1773, their new hallmarks were a crown (for Sheffield, it later became a rose), and an anchor (for Birmingham, the landlocked city 100 miles from the sea!).

Today Birmingham's Assay Office is the busiest in the world, handling over 12 million items every year. It is due to move from its Victorian home in Newhall Street to new purpose built offices on Icknield Street in the next few years. More than 400 jewellery businesses still work in the area north of Birmingham's city centre, which is still known as the Jewellery Quarter. Its buildings, canals and churches reflect the fortunes of the city as a whole, with wealth, decline and regeneration a continuous theme.

This walk also takes in some of the newer parts of the city centre, with the new library an outstanding feature, alongside Brindley Place and the 1980s Gas Street Basin. The canalside paths take you swiftly and quietly from bustling street to bustling street.

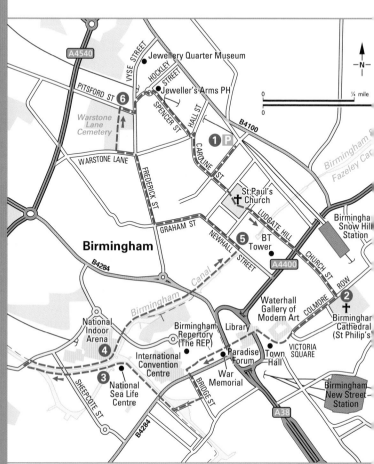

1 From the car park, walk down Northwood Street and go left into Caroline Street. At the end of the street, continue ahead into the churchyard of St Paul's Church, the so-called Jeweller's Church, then walk up Ludgate Hill. Proceed over the Birmingham and Fazeley Canal and cross the footbridge over Great Charles Street Queensway. Continue up Church Street and into Colmore Row to see the impressive Birmingham Cathedral (St Philip's).

2 With your back to the cathedral, turn left and walk along Colmore Row into Victoria Square, passing by the Museum and Art Gallery, Town Hall and Council House. Bear right into Paradise Forum past the Central Library, then cross the walkway into Centenary Square to pass the Hall of Memory war memorial, the new Library for Birmingham and The Rep Theatre. Bear left, across Broad Street, into Bridge Street. Go right in 100yds (91m) to descend to the Worcester and Birmingham Canal, and the Gas

Street Basin. Go left past The James Brindley and cross the canal, via a mooring pontoon and a footbridge, before going right along the tow path past The Tap and Spile pub and beneath Broad Street to Water's Edge, passing the National Sea Life Centre in Brindley Place.

3 Continue ahead over a footbridge and beneath a footbridge numbered 68, along the tow path beneath Sheepcote Street Bridge to St Vincent Bridge. Cross it and descend to the tow path on the other side of the Birmingham Main Line Canal, heading back towards the city centre.

4 Bear left at the Old Turn Junction and walk along the tow path on the left-hand bank of the Birmingham and Fazeley Canal, passing the National Indoor Arena and beneath Tindal Bridge – ahead is the British Telecom Tower. Descend past a flight of eight canal locks and, just before the ninth lock, go left through a gap in the wall and up steps, signed 'Jewellery Quarter', and into Newhall Street.

5 Go left along Newhall Street which becomes Graham Street, then right along Frederick Street past the Argent Centre to see the Jewellery Quarter clock tower. Turn left into Warstone Lane, then just after passing the gateway to the Warstone Lane Cemetery go right up a pathway into the cemetery, past the catacombs, to Pitsford Street.

6 Go right to Vyse Street, then left to the main Jewellery Quarter. Continue right into Hockley Street and then go to the right of The Jewellers Arms pub down Spencer Street. Bear right into Caroline Street, then go left to return along Northwood Street to the car park.

WHERE TO EAT AND DRINK As you pass close to St Paul's Square, call in at The Rope Walk for a pint and a snack – look out for the chef's special. Children are welcome. There are numerous eating places around Brindley Place and the Gas Street Basin. In the Jewellery Quarter, seek out the Hylton Café in Hylton Street for no-nonsense traditional British cafe food served with panache.

••••

WHAT TO SEE Narrowboats line up along the wharves that extend from the Gas Street Basin. Boats stop here from all over the English canal network. Now mostly leisure craft, some of the more exotic looking ones are residential. If you have the chance, why not help a boat's passage through the nine locks on the Birmingham and Fazeley Canal. It can take over an hour to travel the few hundred yards from one end of the flight to the other.

••••

WHILE YOU'RE THERE There are many distractions on this route, but younger visitors will enjoy the National Sea Life Centre at Water's Edge, Brindley Place. It's a children's paradise with over 60 displays, including an Otter Sanctuary and Kingdom of the Seahorses. You can also take a boat trip around the canals on one of several waterbus tours.

Overleaf: 'Spirit & Enterprise' sculpture in Centenary Square (Walk 10)

A Loop from Studley Priory

DISTANCE 5 miles (8km)	MINIMUM TIME 2hrs 15min		

ASCENT/GRADIENT 49ft (15m) ▲ ▲ ▲   LEVEL OF DIFFICULTY ✚✚✚

PATHS Field paths and parkland

LANDSCAPE Gentle rolling countryside

SUGGESTED MAP AA Leisure Map 18 Worcester & The Malverns

START/FINISH Grid reference: SP 071637

DOG FRIENDLINESS Under control at all times

PARKING Pool Road car park, Studley

PUBLIC TOILETS Bottom of High Street, Studley

Although mentioned in the Doomsday Book, very little of ancient Studley remains. The village is built on the old Roman Ryknild Street, which became the main turnpike into Birmingham in 1721. The River Arrow still meanders gently through pastureland below the residential areas.

The mill, an old castle, manor house and church are the only old buildings to survive. Washford Mill has become a public house. The present extraordinary neo-Norman and neo-Gothic Studley Castle was actually built in 1834 as the home of the Goodricke family, and is now a prestigious hotel. Of its 13th-century predecessor nothing remains. The manor house, which is now called Mountbatten House, used to be the headquarters of the Royal Life Saving Society before it moved down the road to Broom, near Alcester. The 700-year-old Church of the Nativity of the Blessed Virgin Mary, on the other side of the river away from the village, features a Norman door, an old rood, some ancient stairs and a stone coffin lid displaying a superb cross. A fascinating brass relates the story of a commendable 17th-century local man who left money for 48 penny loaves for the poor to be distributed every Sunday.

STUDLEY'S TRADE AND INDUSTRY

Needle-making became the main occupation in Studley from the early 17th century, when Elizabeth I allowed a group of Hugenot refugees from France to settle in the area. They brought with them the craft of precision-making needles, which had been developed by Continental manufacturers in the late medieval period. Their expertise helped the local industry develop and soon Studley was one of the largest producers of needles in Britain and known worldwide. From the mid-19th century, surgical needles were greatly in demand. By the end of the 19th century industrial techniques had taken over and there were more than 3,000 workers involved in the needle-making business. Since then the industry has declined, though there is still the need for precision needles and they continue to be made in some of the local factories. It is this industry we must thank for Studley having more public houses than most villages – to supply refreshment to the factory workers.

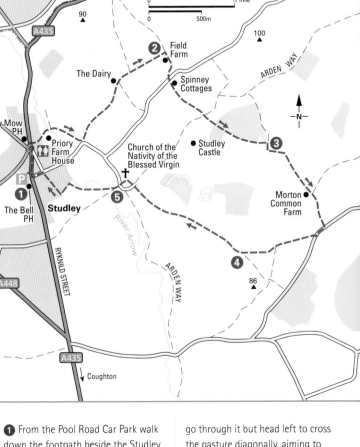

❶ From the Pool Road Car Park walk down the footpath beside the Studley Community Infants School and continue ahead down Needle Close to the Alcester road, then go left to the roundabout. Cross over the road and go down the drive to Priory Court, then via a kissing gate on a footpath to the left of houses. Cross the footbridge over the River Arrow. Go through a kissing gate and bear right to another into a large field, aiming towards a third kissing gate at the corner of the field opposite. Don't

go through it but head left to cross the pasture diagonally, aiming to the left of a field gate in the hedge to a waymarker, then go right alongside the field hedge for about 0.5 miles (800m).

❷ Through a kissing gate and then a hand gate, go right between the buildings of Field Farm and walk along the farm drive. In about 100yds (91m), go right through a gate crossing the corner of the field onto Hardwick Lane via a kissing gate. Cross the lane and, through a gate, walk between Spinney Cottages, then through a kissing gate. Continue ahead over parkland until you come to a driveway near some glasshouses, reaching it via three hand gates. Cross the driveway, go through a handgate and walk to the right of a cottage to enter the wood via two gates. Follow the footpath through the trees and through another gate, then continue ahead by the field-edge until you reach the end of the woodland. Join a farm track, passing a pond on the right.

③ Drawing level with a pond on the left, go right on a track and after 90 paces, go left across the field, aiming for an oak tree. Through the hedge gap, cross the next cultivated field diagonally to a footbridge. Go through a gate, continue alongside a wire fence to a gate, then alongside a hedge, to pass to the left of Morton Common Farm. Reaching the farm drive, follow it to a road. Go right along the road for about 150yds (137m), then right again over a footbridge and go half left through a young wood. At the farm gate, bear right and walk alongside the stream until you reach a farm track.

④ Through a field gate continue right along the track. In about 0.5 miles (800m), it arcs right; turn left here by an old oak to cross the middle of the field, then continue along a hedge path towards Studley's Church of the Nativity of the Blessed Virgin Mary. Go through the overflow graveyard via two handgates, and enter the main churchyard via another, passing the church and leaving via the gate with the lamp over it onto a lane.

⑤ Go briefly left, and cross the lane to go through a kissing gate. Descend through pastureland, cross the footbridge over the River Arrow, then bear right and walk along the river bank towards Studley. A kissing gate leads into the end of Wickham Road. Head left along the side of the housing estate and bear right into Gunners Lane. Continue ahead, and after a path section go left up Castle Road to the Alcester road. Cross and go briefly right and then left to ascend Needle Close, to return to the car park at the start of the walk.

WHERE TO EAT AND DRINK You will be guaranteed a warm welcome at the popular 400-year-old Barley Mow on the corner of Birmingham Road in Studley.

● ● ● ●

WHAT TO SEE The humps in the field across the lane from Studley's church were probably the sites of the simple houses of the original village. The priory, founded in the 12th century, has long gone, and all that remains is the house called Priory Farm House, across the Birmingham Road opposite The Barley Mow.

● ● ● ●

WHILE YOU'RE THERE Visit the Church of the Nativity of the Blessed Virgin Mary in Studley, which still has some of its original Norman features, such as the north wall – a fine example of herringbone masonry. It's an unusually long way out of the village, but was originally surrounded by houses.

Around the Roman Town of Alcester

DISTANCE 5.5 miles (8.8km)	MINIMUM TIME 2hrs 15min	
ASCENT/GRADIENT 269ft (82m) ▲▲▲	LEVEL OF DIFFICULTY +++	
PATHS Pavements, field paths, woodland tracks and farm lanes		
LANDSCAPE Gentle rolling farmland, woodland and rural town		
SUGGESTED MAP AA Leisure Map 18 Worcester & The Malverns		
START/FINISH Grid reference: SP 088572		
DOG FRIENDLINESS Under control at all times		
PARKING Bleachfield Street car park, Alcester		
PUBLIC TOILETS Bulls Head Yard car park, Alcester		

Alcester is one of the most delightful towns in Warwickshire. This former Roman settlement has sadly lost its ancient abbey, but the abbot's splendid ivory crozier, which was discovered in the rectory garden, is now displayed in the British Museum. From time to time new Roman relics also come to light, such as the Roman milestone commemorating the Emperor Constantine (AD 306–337), which was excavated in the town in 1966. The Romano-British town, which flourished between the 2nd and 4th centuries, is now completely covered by the modern town.

MAJOR TRANSPORT ARTERY

Following the turnpiking of the Stratford to Alcester road in 1753, Alcester became a busy stopping point on the main stagecoach route linking London and Holyhead via Shrewsbury. Few of the town's old coaching inns survived the developments of the 1960s, but the Swan, Bear and White Lion are reminders of those days.

BLOOMING ALCESTER

The town centre is now bypassed and so Alcester has had the space to spruce itself up. As a national winner of the Britain in Bloom competition, the residents adorn its streets each year with beautiful flowers, making the High Street particularly attractive. The great tower of St Nicholas dominates the centre, with its clock face set at an angle on the corner of its tower. The Market Hall was originally built in 1618, when it was simply a pillared edifice, but a timber-framed upper storey was added in 1641. In 1874 the arches were filled in and today it is occupied by the Town Hall.

FOREST OF ARDEN

The walk takes you through the old part of Alcester and down Malt Mill Lane into Oversley Green. Beautiful Oversley Wood is a remnant of the original Forest of Arden, and if you walk through here in spring you will be greeted by a carpet of bluebells and may even spot a shy muntjac deer.

The route goes close to the delightful villages of Exhall and Wixford, with their black-and-white buildings, then returns over Primrose Hill, which rises 350ft (107m) above the Arrow Valley, offering a fine view of Ragley Hall (see While You're There) to the left. Once over the busy A46 road you will pass several beautiful thatched cottages as you walk down Primrose Lane on the way back into Oversley Green.

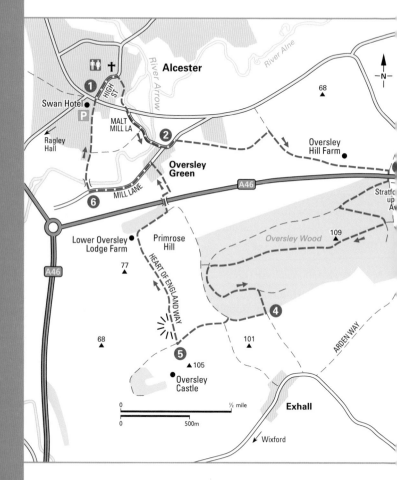

❶ From the car park enter Bleachfield Street and go left to the old Stratford Road. Cross the road and wander up High Street. Bear right past impressive St Nicholas Church and, at the corner of the road, turn right down Malt Mill Lane. At the bottom of the lane, go left through the public gardens and follow the tarmac footpath by the side of the River Arrow to reach the

old Stratford Road again. Cross the road and go down the lane opposite into Oversley Green village, crossing the bridge over the River Arrow.

❷ Keep left through the village on Stratford Road, and 80yds (73m) after passing a road to the right, go right along a hedged footpath behind a row of houses. Cross a field via two kissing gates and walk past a golf driving range, to reach a kissing gate at a junction of paths. Do not go through it but go right here along the field edge, then through a field gate and across pastureland to join a track. Follow this through a kissing gate below Oversley Hill Farm to reach a Severn Trent sub station.

3 Continue ahead across a stile and through a gate to go right, under the A46 road bridge, and bear right through the gateway into Oversley Wood. Take the metalled track into the wood for about 400yds (366m), then go left. In a further 400yds (366m) the metalled track arcs right. In 50yds (46m), at a path crossroads, go right on a grass path steeply uphill and continue westwards over the crest of the hill. Descend past a viewpoint bench back to the main metalled track. Now go left for 650yds (594m), then right at a bench onto a wide path to leave the wood over a stile.

4 Go right through dense vegetation and walk along the edge of Oversley Wood to its corner. Continue ahead along the hedged track until you reach a farm lane, with Oversley Castle on the hillock to the left.

5 Go right along the lane and join the Heart of England Way. Walk up the lane towards some large grain silos by the side of Lower Oversley Lodge Farm. From the farm complex go right along the concrete lane and left through a handgate down to the footbridge over the busy A46. Cross and walk down Primrose Lane, passing a thatched house. At the T-junction go left along Mill Lane for about 650yds (594m).

6 After passing a fourth mobile home, go right down a path and cross a footbridge over the River Arrow. Continuing ahead, the path becomes a lane by houses, with allotments to the right. Walk up Bleachfield Street back to the car park.

WHERE TO EAT AND DRINK Alcester has a large number of public houses and eating places. The Bleachfield Street car park is at the rear of The Swan Hotel, a regular drinking hole for walkers. You'll be made very welcome and can enjoy great home-cooked meals at reasonable prices and a good selection of beers.

● ● ● ●

WHAT TO SEE The lovely Church of St Milburga, on the edge of Wixford village, is tucked away up a high banked lane and is almost hidden from view by the oldest yew tree in Warwickshire. Look especially for the 1411 Crewe brass, which lies on top of a tomb in the south chapel.

● ● ● ●

WHILE YOU'RE THERE Take the opportunity to visit Ragley Hall, along the Evesham Road, set in 400 acres (165ha) of parkland. The home of the Marquess and Marchioness of Hertford, it was designed by Robert Hooke in 1680, and is one of the earliest and most handsome of England's great Palladian houses. The magnificent great hall contains some outstanding baroque plasterwork by James Gibbs and a large mural up the stairway. The stables house a carriage collection, and 'Capability' Brown designed the gardens.

Overleaf: A thatched cottage on Primrose Lane , Oversley Green (Walk 12)

On the Avon Valley Footpath from Bidford

DISTANCE 7 miles (11.3km)	MINIMUM TIME 3hrs
ASCENT/GRADIENT 190ft (58m) ▲▲▲	LEVEL OF DIFFICULTY ✦✦✦

PATHS Field paths, farm tracks and country lanes

LANDSCAPE Riverside and rolling countryside

SUGGESTED MAP OS Explorer 205 Stratford-upon-Avon & Evesham

START/FINISH Grid reference: SP 098518

DOG FRIENDLINESS On lead at all times

PARKING Car park southeast of roundabout in Bidford-on-Avon

PUBLIC TOILETS At recreation ground

William Shakespeare (1564–1616) is believed to have been a regular visitor to Bidford-on-Avon. The former 13th-century Falcon Inn, opposite the church, was one of his favourite taverns. He reputedly got drunk at the inn and slept it off under a crab apple tree on his way back to his home in Stratford-upon-Avon. He recounts his drinking exploits in the local villages in a rhyme that finishes '...Papish Wicksford, Beggarly Broom and Drunken Bidford'. Sadly, the old inn fell into disrepair and was subsequently renovated and turned into flats some years ago. The crab apple tree has long disappeared.

HISTORIC BIDFORD

Bidford can trace its origins back to Saxon times when it was called Byda's Ford, though Roman legions had earlier tramped the area. The ford would have been on their great Ryknild Street. As you stroll back along the river bank into Bidford-on-Avon you'll enjoy a superb view of St Lawrence's Church and the mainly 15th-century Bidford Bridge. Lean on its parapet and watch the placid waters of the Avon flow by the willow beds below – this is Shakespeare country at its very best.

The fine 13th-century Church of St Lawrence stands above the River Avon. Its first incumbent was Rogenus Capellanno in 1260, and inside you can see a beautiful church plate that was presented to the church in 1660 by Duchess Dudley. In the 19th century the village became known locally for its cockfighting, wrestling and swordsmanship.

This walk takes you along the River Avon, passing a lovely weir at Barton where The Cottage of Content pub is a famous local drinking hole for walkers. You may wish to continue into Welford-on-Avon to see the timbered black-and-white thatched cottages that line its streets. Your return is along the Heart of England Way.

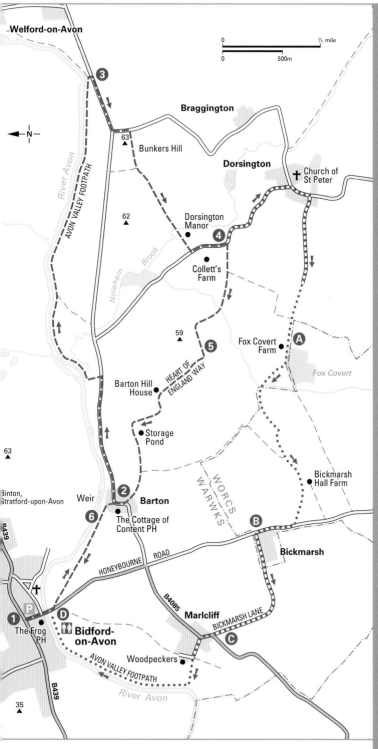

Welford-on-Avon

0   ½ mile

0   500m

—N—

Braggington

Bunkers Hill

Dorsington

63

River Avon

AVON VALLEY FOOTPATH

62

Noleham Brook

Dorsington Manor

Church of St Peter

Collett's Farm

Fox Covert Farm

A

Fox Covert

59

5

HEART OF ENGLAND WAY

Barton Hill House

Bickmarsh Hall Farm

63

Storage Pond

WORCS WARWKS

Binton, Stratford-upon-Avon

Weir

2

Barton

B

B439

6

The Cottage of Content PH

Bickmarsh

HONEYBOURNE   ROAD

B4085

Marlcliff

BICKMARSH LANE

C

1

P

D

Bidford-on-Avon

The Frog PH

AVON VALLEY FOOTPATH

Woodpeckers

B439

River Avon

35

❶ Cross Bidford Bridge and go left through a kissing gate by a farm gate. Follow the Heart of England Way waymarkers through three kissing gates over a series of fields to the River Avon. Continue by the riverside until you reach a weir and lock gates, then go right up to the road in the hamlet of Barton – The Cottage of Content pub is on the right.

❷ Leave the Heart of England Way and head left along the road for about 0.5 miles (800m). Go left through a gateway opposite Willow Cottage, down to the river's edge, and follow the Avon Valley Footpath by the side of the Avon for the next 1.5 miles (2.4km). After passing two benches, bear right to a kissing gate and climb the steps up Cress Hill until you come to a road, through a kissing gate.

❸ Turn right along the road, bearing left at the road junction by Bunkers Hill. In 125yds (114m), go right through a kissing gate and take the footpath on the left of the field hedge. This leads, via four gates and two drives, past a swimming pool, then continues over a series of fields and one gate until through a kissing gate you cross a footbridge over Noleham Brook, passing to the right of Dorsington Manor to reach the Dorsington road. Go left along the road for 300yds (274m) to where it bears left.

❹ Go right to rejoin the Heart of England Way, taking a track past Collett's Farm to a gate. Through this continue ahead, and follow the waymarkers as the track crosses a stile to skirt a young copse and lake, then through a gate and over a footbridge, before continuing ahead to follow a hedge uphill. Go left at a waymark post and follow the path for about 250yds (229m).

❺ Turn right at a waymark post and walk towards Barton Hill House. Pass to the left of the buildings and bear left, then shortly right. Follow the track past a large storage pond. Continue on the track as it arcs right and gently descends into Barton. At the road, go right and then ahead through a gate by The Cottage of Content pub, and take the wide track down to the Avon.

❻ Walk along the riverside footpath, retracing your steps back to the car park in Bidford-on-Avon.

WHERE TO EAT AND DRINK The Cottage of Content pub at Barton is a regular stopping-off place for walkers on the Heart of England Way. At The Frog pub, along the High Street in Bidford-on-Avon, you can enjoy a pleasant bar snack by the river.

● ● ● ●

WHAT TO SEE Linger in the 'Bard's villages' of Barton, Dorsington and Marlcliff and take time to enjoy the attractive cottages. Marlcliff, by the River Avon, is a charming mix of old, thatched buildings and more modern ones that blend in perfectly.

● ● ● ●

WHILE YOU'RE THERE Climb the 700-year-old tower of Bidford's St Lawrence's Church. It rises above a small avenue of lime trees, and from the top there are exceptional views of the town's beautiful eight-arched bridge and the Avon, with the Cotswold Hills behind.

From Bidford-on-Avon to Dorsington and Marlcliff

DISTANCE 8.5 miles (13.7km)   MINIMUM TIME 3hrs 30min

ASCENT/GRADIENT 246ft (75m) ▲▲   LEVEL OF DIFFICULTY +++

SEE MAP AND INFORMATION PANEL FOR WALK 13

Leave Walk 13 at Point ❹ and continue along the road into the village of Dorsington, sparing time to walk around the village green and see the curious 18th-century Church of St Peter. Rest a while at the metal seat that encircles a lovely old oak tree by the church.

Walk past the road junction by the church for 150yds (137m), then just past the schoolhouse go right up a quiet lane into open countryside. After 0.5 miles (800m), continue on a track between hedges until you get close to Fox Covert Farm. Pass to the right of Fox Covert (Point Ⓐ) and, where the track arcs left, cross a footbridge and stile and continue in a northwest direction beside a hedge. Over a footbridge arc left, then right at a wood. Cross a footbridge, and after about 100 paces enter the wood via a footbridge with a stile at each end. Skirt pheasant enclosures, and beyond the wood continue across a cultivated field until you come to the drive to Bickmarsh Hall Farm.

Go left along the driveway, passing to the right of the major farm complex and on to Honeybourne Road. Go right along the grass verge of the road for about 300yds (274m), past the roadside houses in Bickmarsh (Point Ⓑ).

Go left along Bickmarsh Sixteen Acres Lane until you reach the B4085 on the edge of the hamlet of Marlcliff. You will pass a number of houses before reaching cultivated farmland where there is a fine view ahead of the surrounding countryside. When you descend to the road junction, go right along the B4085 for some 90yds (82m), then turn left into Marlcliff (Point Ⓒ).

Follow the lane, The Bank, into the centre. Where the dead-end lane bends right, continue ahead, passing by a tiny thatched cottage and the corner house called Woodpeckers, and go down a lane towards the River Avon.

Reaching the river, bear right over a footbridge and through a gate and take the Avon Valley Footpath along the banks of the Avon, passing through a kissing gate and over a plank footbridge before coming to the recreation ground, via another plank footbridge. Through this you can exit onto Bidford Bridge. Go left over the bridge (Point Ⓓ) and complete the walk by crossing the road and strolling up to the car park.

A Circuit from the Earlswood Lakes

DISTANCE 5.5 miles (8.8km)   MINIMUM TIME 2hrs 15min

ASCENT/GRADIENT 98ft (30m) ▲▲▲   LEVEL OF DIFFICULTY ✦✦✦

PATHS Lakeside paths and field paths

LANDSCAPE Woodland, lakes and rolling countryside

SUGGESTED MAP OS Explorer 220 Birmingham

START/FINISH Grid reference: SP 109739

DOG FRIENDLINESS Off lead on lakeside footpaths, care needed near wildfowl

PARKING Earlswood Lakes (Tanworth in Arden Parish Council) car park

PUBLIC TOILETS Earlswood Lakes Craft Centre

Earlswood is delightfully situated in the Forest of Arden. The three man-made lakes here, known as Terry's Pool, Engine Pool and Windmill Pool, were completed in 1821 to supply water to the nearby Birmingham–Stratford-upon-Avon canal. It took five years to build the reservoirs – at a cost of about £300,000, and using the labour of men captured during the Napoleonic Wars.

NATURAL BY-PRODUCTS

The canal has not been in commercial use since 1936 but, being so close to the sprawling West Midlands conurbation, it has developed into a major leisure facility. This is also true of Earlswood Lakes, where city dwellers can enjoy nature, albeit in a manufactured setting. Visit on a sunny Sunday morning and Windmill Pool will be full of the boats of the Earlswood Lakes Sailing Club, while the banks of the Engine Pool will be covered with anglers. The 10-hectare (25-acre) reservoir has no fewer than 80 timber platforms for anglers, who are keen to catch one of the huge carp that thrive in these waters. Bream, roach and perch can also be found in the other two pools.

A WILDLIFE HAVEN

Terry's Pool is a wildlife reserve that is home to a wealth of birds, mammals and plants. Walkers out close to dusk might see bats, muntjac deer and even otters. You need to be both quiet and patient to catch sight of the latter, though – they are notoriously shy. Watch for their prints in the soft mud on the banks of the reservoirs and streams; they have five webbed toes, although it is common for only four to show up in prints. Otters were driven to the brink of extinction in England in the middle of the 20th century, but numbers have recovered significantly in the last couple of decades. During spring and summer Terry's Pool is a riot of colour, home to the bright flowers of yellow flag iris, great willowherb and betony.

New Fallings Coppice and Clowes Wood contain areas of ancient woodland that are the breeding grounds for an amazing 49 species of bird. These include all three species of woodpecker that are found in England, along with several tit species, warblers, kestrels, tawny owls and even the elusive woodcock – a large, dumpy-looking wading bird with short legs and a long bill.

The walk starts from Terry's Pool and takes in these woods, as well as farmland, a golf course and country roads, before returning for a lakeside stroll.

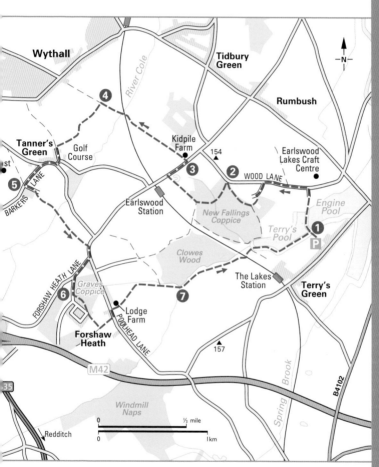

❶ From the car park, go through a kissing gate and over a footbridge to cross the embankment between the lakes. After a metal bridge, bear right and then left over a wooden footbridge. Continue to Wood Lane. Go left for 400yds (366m), then left along a campsite driveway. Walk past

the log cabin, and at the woodland edge go right over a footbridge and bear left, along the side of New Fallings Coppice.

❷ Cross a stile, turn left and bear right at a fork. After a footbridge, keep straight ahead. Just before the path swings left, leave it by bearing right to join a trail along the coppice boundary to a fence gap. Through this, follow a path across a field. This becomes a hedged path that leads to a road. Turn right along the road for 200yds (183m).

❸ Just before Kidpile Farm, go left through a gap beside a gate. Initially the path is to the left of the hedge, then enters trees via two kissing gates and a footbridge, before continuing on the right. After a kissing gate, bear half right to pass, via another kissing gate, under the railway. Continue up the side of a field, soon joining a hedged path beside Fulford Heath Golf Club.

❹ Go left through a kissing gate and take the waymarked footpath across the golf course. After the maintenance yard, bear right to a kissing gate. Through this, bear left. Reaching a road at the golf club entrance, turn right towards Wythall. After 125yds (114m), go left down Barkers Lane.

❺ In a further 250yds (229m) go left along a driveway signed 'Forshaw Heath' and right over a stile. Over the next stile, cross a field to a footbridge. Once over this, bear right. Cross a plank footbridge and walk straight across a large field. Turn right along Forshaw Heath Lane, right at the next junction and then left into Juggins Lane.

❻ In 300yds (274m), turn left through Graves Coppice, exiting via a footbridge. Continue through a field and, after the second stile, turn left to Poolhead Lane. Go left for 100yds (91m), then right over a stile by Lodge Farm. Bear half left after a stile, cross a footbridge and then recross via a second bridge. Go left and then through a kissing gate straight ahead to walk beside Clowes Wood.

❼ After about 0.5 miles (800m), having crossed two gated footbridges, go through a gate and bear right to cross the railway. After a kissing gate, take the footpath ahead to a stile. Go through a kissing gate and over a footbridge, then turn right to emerge beside Terry's Pool. Continue for 700yds (640m), then go right to return to the car park.

WHERE TO EAT AND DRINK The Reservoir Inn, at the junction of the B4102 (Solihull) and Earlswood roads, offers excellent food and is popular with local walking groups (children and dogs allowed). Light meals and refreshments are available at The Manor House Tea Room, at Earlswood Lakes Craft Centre.

● ● ● ●

WHAT TO SEE Children will enjoy the nearby Umberslade Children's Farm (open daily from mid-February until Christmas Eve). Here they can get up close to the animals, including lambs, pigs, donkeys, shire horses and goats. Daily events include supervised bottle-feeding and holding the animals, pony rides and tractor and trailer rides.

● ● ● ●

WHILE YOU'RE THERE Earlswood Lakes Craft Centre (closed Mondays) has a fascinating selection of small shops selling ceramics, glass novelty garden and household ornaments, silk and dried flowers, horse supplies, upholstery and jewellery.

A Longer Ramble Through Sutton Park

DISTANCE 8 miles (12.9km)	MINIMUM TIME 3hrs

ASCENT/GRADIENT 230ft (70m) ▲▲▲   LEVEL OF DIFFICULTY +++

PATHS Footpaths, tracks and road in parkland

LANDSCAPE Undulating parkland

SUGGESTED MAP OS Explorer 220 Birmingham

START/FINISH Grid reference: SP 113962

DOG FRIENDLINESS Off lead in park

PARKING Visitor centre car park, Sutton Park, accessed via Town Gate

PUBLIC TOILETS Visitor centre, Sutton Park

Sutton Park comprises 2,400 acres (970ha) of wild and wooded countryside of moorland, meadows, lakes and groves and is one of the largest urban parks in the country. The ancient Roman Ryknild Street runs across one corner of the park, and the Normans once hunted deer here. William Shakespeare had kinsmen at Sutton and is likely to have visited the site. One of his famous characters, Sir John Falstaff, probably brought his Ragged Army here, for he declared to Bardolph: 'Get thee before to Coventry; fill me a bottle of sack; our soldiers shall march through. We'll to Sutton Coldfield tonight.' (*King Henry IV, Part I*)

BIRMINGHAM'S LUNG

In 1997 English Nature designated Sutton Park a National Nature Reserve (NNR) in an effort to preserve this wonderful landscape. Although it is now surrounded on all sides by residential properties, it remains an important area for Birmingham and the local Sutton Coldfield community. It's a valuable space in an otherwise congested region and offers many leisure pursuits – for joggers, kite-fliers, cyclists and walkers. However, it is still possible to escape from the crowds and find peace and quiet.

It is the diversity of habitats in the park which earned its NNR status. Many areas, like the heathland, wetland and ancient forest, represent habitats that were once widespread but have now completely disappeared from the rest of the West Midlands. For this reason, it is the home of a large number of resident birds, as well as providing an important stopover for migrants and other visitors. Around the pools you might see tufted duck, pochard and even snipe, especially near Longmoor Pool. It is hoped that red kites and other vanished species will one day return.

The nearby market town of Sutton Coldfield was important in the Middle Ages and owes a great deal to local benefactor John Veysey, who became bishop of Exeter in 1519. He lived at Moor

Hall, north of the town and now a hotel, and built a number of notable buildings in and around the town. He also founded a school and paved the streets. Veysey is buried in Holy Trinity Church and there is a fine effigy of him on his tomb. It depicts him as a young man, even though he is reputed to have lived to the ripe old age of 103. The church also contains some interesting old brasses. In particular there is one of Josias Bull in a gown of fur, along with small brasses of his five children. William Wilson, a mason for Sir Christopher Wren, carved the marble busts of Henry Pudsey and his wife.

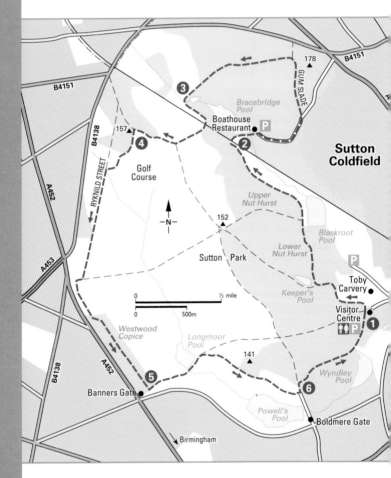

❶ Walk from the car park to the entrance road, and go left and shortly right at a five-way junction to follow the tarmac lane up to Keeper's Pool. At the corner of the pool turn right and follow its edge, continuing northwards uphill through the trees on a path until you descend to reach Blackroot Pool. Walk close to the left edge of the pool for about 220yds (201m), then follow the path bearing left (northwest) and keep ahead through the woodland of Upper Nut Hurst. In about 0.5 miles (800m), bear right and cross the railway bridge, via two gates, to get to Bracebridge Pool.

② Turn right along the edge of the pool, and at the end bear right along a track just before The Boathouse Restaurant. Continue along the tarmac lane and through the car park until you reach a T-junction by housing. Turn left, and in 150yds (137m) leave the road and go left by a large oak tree on a wide path, which soon bears right by ancient oaks in the woodland of Gum Slade. Continue ahead to a junction of paths, then go left and up to a grassy clearing. Cross it and continue ahead on a gravel track. Where this bears right continue ahead, ignoring minor cross paths, and descending gently. Maintain your direction then continue ahead on a track that arcs left and descends to cross a footbridge at the end of Bracebridge Pool.

③ Bear left, following the track into the woods. It then arcs right to cross the railway line again, via two handgates. Keep on the wide track until you reach a road, then go right for 500yds (457m) up to a parking area on the left.

④ At the far end of the parking area turn left by a post, and take the path that dives through the trees and passes a golf green. Now keep to the left of the fairway, descending to a small stream. Here turn left on to a straight path flanked by silver birches. This is the Roman Ryknild Street. Continue, initially within the golf course, but later across heath, until you reach a track leading to an exit. Turn right and then left just before the exit handgate and follow the path through the trees of Westwood Coppice until you come to the car park by Banners Gate.

⑤ Bear left up the road, passing to the right of Longmoor Pool. About 100yds (91m) beyond the end of the pool, turn right along a path. Join a path from the left and continue on it, passing to the right of a copse of silver birches. Soon you walk alongside a fence and trees, drop through a tree belt and cross an open grass area close to Powell's Pool to reach the roadway, via the car park near Boldmere Gate.

⑥ Go left at the road, then soon bear right, along the edge of Wyndley Wood, and join a tarmac lane. In 150yds (137m) bear right at a four-way lane junction on to a straight road that descends to pass a footbridge and ford at the end of Wyndley Pool. Continue ahead to return to the visitor centre at the start of the walk.

WHERE TO EAT AND DRINK There are a number of places in Sutton Park with cafes and kiosks at the various park entrances. The Toby Carvery at Town Gate serves food all day. The Boathouse Restaurant at Bracebridge Pool is a bistro serving good value table d'hôte lunches.

● ● ● ●

WHAT TO SEE The beautiful Bracebridge Pool was built for Sir Ralph Bracebridge in order to maintain a plentiful supply of fish. In 1419, he obtained a lease on the manor and chase of Sutton Coldfield from the Earl of Warwick.

Black-and-White Buildings in Welford

DISTANCE 3 miles (4.8km)	MINIMUM TIME 1hr 15min
ASCENT/GRADIENT 49ft (15m) ▲▲▲	LEVEL OF DIFFICULTY ✦✦✦
PATHS Village footpaths and field paths	
LANDSCAPE Residential village area	
SUGGESTED MAP OS Explorer 205 Stratford-upon-Avon & Evesham	
START/FINISH Grid reference: SP 148522	
DOG FRIENDLINESS Under control at all times	
PARKING Near Bell Inn, Welford-on-Avon	
PUBLIC TOILETS None on route	

This walk takes you on a journey back in time – to the delightful black-and-white villages of Welford-on-Avon and Weston-on-Avon, with their links to William Shakespeare.

Picturesque Welford-on-Avon, a frequent winner of best kept village competitions, was established in Saxon times by the monks of Deerhurst Abbey (near Tewkesbury, in Gloucestershire). There must be more black-and-white thatched cottages here than almost any other village in England. Three particularly stunning examples are Ten Penny Cottage, the Owl Pen and Daffodil Cottage. Welford also boasts three old pubs – The Shakespeare, The Bell Inn and The Four Alls, all of which welcome walkers. In the porch of The Four Alls is a painting that depicts four characters:

'The king who rules over all
The parson who prays for all
The soldier who fights for all
The farmer who pays for all.'

MAYPOLE TRADITION

Since the 14th century there has been a 65-ft (20m) high maypole on the village green. It must have been taken down some time after the Civil War, when such frivolities were made illegal, but seems to have been restored soon after. Following a lightning strike, the original wooden pole was replaced by an aluminium ship's mast. Welford is proud of its traditions, and the village children still dance around the maypole in July each year.

THE SHAKESPEARE CONNECTIONS

William Shakespeare has connections with neighbouring Weston-on-Avon. John Trapp was vicar in this tiny village in the 1660s. He was also a master at Stratford Grammar School for a time, and it is believed that he and his wife knew the Shakespeare family.

Welford's church has a register which records the flooding of the River Avon in 1588 – this was due to the same storm that wrecked the Spanish Armada. Joseph Green, the vicar here in 1735, discovered and made copies of Shakespeare's will, one of which is now held in the British Museum.

In the sanctuary of the church two fighting men are depicted in full armour. Sir John Greville, of nearby Milcote Manor, is shown with his head resting on a horned sheep and flowers at his feet, while his son, who fought in the Battle of the Spurs in 1513, wears an heraldic coat and holds his hands in prayer.

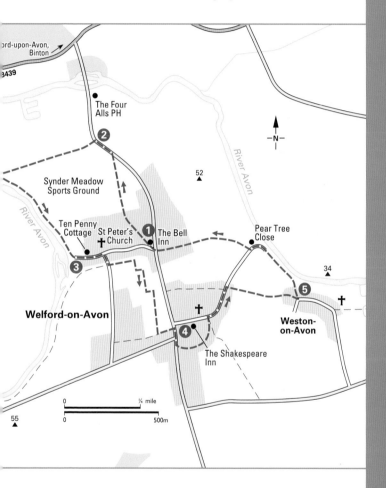

❶ Leave The Bell Inn car park, come out onto the main road in Welford and go left down the footpath at the side of the parking area. At the end of the path, near Daffodil Cottage, go right along a footpath past the back of some houses and through a kissing gate until you come to the end of Church Lane, by Applegarth House. Continue through the gate and follow a green path at the back of more houses to reach the main road once again, then go left along the pavement for about 100yds (91m).

2 Go left again into the entrance gate of Synder Meadow Sports Ground. Walk along the track, then through a kissing gate into the sports ground, and soon out via a gate in the fence on the right to continue along the footpath down to the River Avon. At the river, go left and follow the bank for 500yds (457m).

3 Go through the kissing gate and over a footbridge at the end of the field and left up Boat Lane, lined with beautiful old thatched black-and-white cottages. Look out for Ten Penny Cottage. Near the top of the lane is St Peter's Church; go right here along Headland Road. Opposite Mill Lane, turn left along a footpath at the back of houses. After a kissing gate you will pass by the extension to the graveyard of St Peter's Church and continue to a junction of paths. Keep ahead here, and at the next junction go left and through a kissing gate. Walk up to the High Street to emerge opposite the Maypole general store, near the famous maypole.

4 Turn right along the pavement for 100 paces, then cross over and go down another waymarked footpath, past more beautiful thatched cottages and through a kissing gate. Walk through Pool Close to Chapel Street (the chapel is on the left). Go right along Chapel Street, then right again through a kissing gate along a footpath just after Millers Close. Go through another kissing gate and walk along the field-edge towards Weston-on-Avon.

5 At the crossroads keep ahead to descend a bridlepath set just above the River Avon. Follow it as it arcs left to come out on Duck Lane by another superb thatched house called Pear Tree Close. At the next residential drive, go right up the hedged path and walk up to High Street, where you will emerge at the junction with Church Street. The Bell Inn is on the right.

WHERE TO EAT AND DRINK There are three pubs in Welford-upon-Avon. The Bell Inn, at the start, is colourful with flowers during the summer months. The Shakespeare Inn lies just beyond the maypole in Chapel Street, and The Four Alls is close to the weir and Welford Bridge. They can all get very busy during the summer when many visitors come to admire the flower-adorned village.

● ● ● ●

WHAT TO SEE Visit the neighbouring village of Binton to see the memorial to Captain Robert Falcon Scott. The famous explorer, whose brother-in-law, Lloyd Bruce, was the vicar in Binton, spent time here before his final expedition to the South Pole in 1912. Binton commemorated the exploits of the great man in the church's west window.

● ● ● ●

WHILE YOU'RE THERE St Peter's Church in Welford has a Saxon font bowl and carved wooden screen dedicated to the 'Fallen of the First World War'. In nearby Weston's 15th-century church you can find out about the 'Wicked Loddy'. Was he really the notorious Lodvic Greville, son of Sir Edward Greville of Milcote Manor, pressed to death with stones in 1589 for murder?

Henley and the Stratford Canal

DISTANCE 5.5 miles (8.8km)		MINIMUM TIME 2hrs	

ASCENT/GRADIENT 180ft (55m) ▲▲▲   LEVEL OF DIFFICULTY ✚✚✚

PATHS Field paths, farm tracks and tow path

LANDSCAPE Rolling countryside

SUGGESTED MAP OS Explorer 220 Birmingham

START/FINISH Grid reference: SP 152658

DOG FRIENDLINESS Off lead along tow path, otherwise under control

PARKING Prince Harry Road car park, Henley-in-Arden

PUBLIC TOILETS Station Road, Henley-in-Arden

This walk takes you over the top of the Mount for a great view over Henley-in-Arden, and then descends on country lanes past Preston Bagot Manor House on the way to the Stratford-upon-Avon Canal.

Henley-in-Arden has a superb mile-long (1.6km) street which offers a glimpse of the medieval world. It is lined with mostly 15th-, 16th- and 17th-century timber-framed buildings, with roofs at every level, ancient windows and a wide variety of old doors. It has often been described as a museum of English domestic architecture.

LORD OF THE MANOR

Peter de Montfort was Henley's Lord of the Manor until he fell in battle on Evesham Field in 1265. Following the battle, the town was burnt to the ground, but a new Henley rose from the ashes. The town maintains a Court Leet that has jurisdiction over petty offences and civil affairs. While this has been abolished in most towns, the Henley-in-Arden Court Leet has survived and each year the Burgesses elect a High and Low Bailiff, a Mace Bearer, a Constable, an Ale Taster, two Brook Lookers, a Butter Weigher and two Affearors (assessors). These ceremonial roles were dying out by the early 20th century, but were revived in 1915 by the then Lord of the Manor, W J Fieldhouse. His title was later bought by the Pittsburgh millionaire Joseph Hardy, who established a charitable trust which now runs the heritage centre in the town.

MEMORIALS

Peter de Montfort lived at the castle that used to stand behind Beaudesert Church, and the hill is known locally as The Mount in his memory. The church has a memorial tablet to the Revd Richard Jago, father of the esteemed 17th-century poet Richard Jago.

In medieval days the horse ruled the world of transport and coaching inns became a feature of many towns. Three very old inns remain in Henley – The Three Tuns, The Blue Bell and The White

Swan. The White Swan is opposite the Guildhall and was a haunt of local poets, possibly even Shakespeare. It is thought that the 18th-century poet William Shenstone wrote the following elegant piece of verse here:

'Whoe'er has travelled life's dull round,
Where'er his journey may have been
Must sigh to think he still has found
His warmest welcome at an inn.'

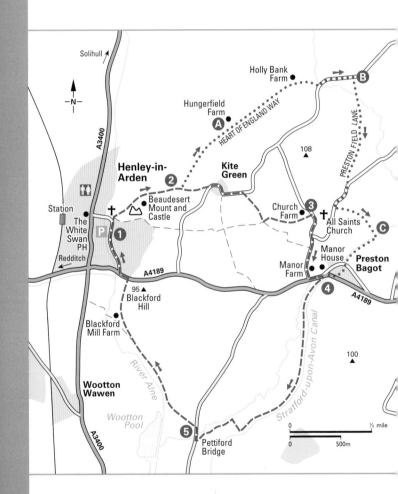

❶ After leaving the car park at the rear, walk through the gardens, cross the footbridge and go left into Alne Close. At the end you come to Beaudesert Lane, opposite Beaudesert Church. Go right through the kissing gate to the right of churchyard, and follow the Heart of England Way for a steep but short ascent to the top of the Mount. Continue over the old earthworks of the former castle of the de Montfort family until you reach the corner of the top far field. Go right over the stile and continue along the footpath that runs to the right of the hedge.

2 In about 220yds (201m), cross a stile and go left over another stile. Diagonally cross the next field to a stile, then follow the path to gate leading onto a lane in Kite Green. Turn right, then go left along the lane for 0.25 miles (400m). Just past Barn View, turn right through a handgate and shortly through a kissing gate onto a footpath, following the left-hand edge of a field. At end of the field go through two kissing gates and proceed in an easterly direction towards Church Farm.

3 After three kissing gates, go through the gate to the right of the farm buildings onto a lane. Turn right and follow the lane, passing by Manor Farm to reach the A4189 Henley–Warwick road. Go left along the road for about 220yds (201m), then cross it.

4 Immediately before the canal bridge, descend onto the tow path of the Stratford-upon-Avon Canal, via two gates, and take this back towards Henley-in-Arden. Continue past canal bridge No. 49. Leave the canal at bridge No. 50 and go right along lane. In 180yds (165m), this bends sharp left, bringing you to a road near the Pettiford Bridge. Turn right over the bridge.

5 In 50yds (46m), go left through a kissing gate into pastureland. The path arcs right, diagonally over a field. Over a plank footbridge and through a kissing gate in the far corner, you reach the banks of the River Alne. Take the riverside path then, at a hedge gap junction, bear right and shortly take the right-hand footpath and proceed ahead, passing to the right of Blackford Mill Farm buildings via a kissing gate and a handgate. Continue on field paths to the left of Blackford Hill to reach the A4189 road in Henley-in-Arden via a kissing gate. Cross the road going left, then right onto Prince Harry Road which leads back to the car park.

WHERE TO EAT AND DRINK There are a number of good pubs in Henley-in-Arden, including three superb old coaching inns. The White Swan, a restored 16th-century coaching inn opposite the Guildhall, is a regular stop-off for walkers completing the 100-mile (161km) Heart of England Way, which passes through its archway. Well-behaved children and dogs are welcome in the bar and the large rear gardens.

• • • •

WHAT TO SEE Make a short detour to see the Norman All Saints Church in Preston Bagot. Enjoy the view from the seat by the church, which carries the message 'Rest and be thankful'. On a summer's day the altar cross becomes ablaze with light as the sun sets behind the hills to the west.

• • • •

WHILE YOU'RE THERE The Stratford-upon-Avon Canal was completed in 1816 to link up with the Worcester and Birmingham Canal at King's Norton. It became derelict, but was saved by a group of canal enthusiasts and has since become a popular leisure facility for boaters, walkers, anglers, canoeists and artists. Note the cast-iron split bridges on the Stratford-upon-Avon Canal – these are an unusual sight in England.

On Byways from Henley to Aston Bagot

DISTANCE 7 miles (11.3km)   MINIMUM TIME 3 hrs

ASCENT/GRADIENT 230ft (70m) ▲▲▲   LEVEL OF DIFFICULTY +++

SEE MAP AND INFORMATION PANEL FOR WALK 18

At Point ❷ on Walk 18 continue ahead to stay on the Heart of England Way. After a 0.25 miles (400m), go right over a stile and cross the next field diagonally to a further stile. Cross this, and go left up a hedged track for 50yds (46m), then right to walk in a northeasterly direction. Go over a farm track with Hungerfield Farm on your left (Point Ⓐ), then continue through two more fields via a kissing gate.

Through a second kissing gate descend towards Holly Bank Farm, passing to its right to reach the Henley–Lowsonford road, via another kissing gate. Go left along the road for about 0.25 miles (400m), then turn right at Willowbrook Barn onto an unclassified county road (Point Ⓑ).

This is Preston Field Lane, and after crossing a ford the track becomes a green lane and then a tarmac road. You will pass a beautiful thatched cottage just before you reach Rookery Lane. Go right along the lane towards Preston Bagot. In about 220yds (201m), go left through a kissing gate opposite Preston Bagot church, enjoying the fine view as you descend fields. The route takes you through a hedge gap and then continues in

a southeasterly direction alongside the right hand hedge to a gate and a footbridge. Go over the footbridge and take a footpath through the trees to reach the tow path of the Stratford-upon-Avon Canal (Point Ⓒ).

The Stratford-upon-Avon Canal was completed in 1816 (see While You're There, Walk 18). In those pioneering days of the Industrial Revolution, canals were a major transport facility, and agricultural goods and limestone were regularly carried by barge to Birmingham. In 1850 the Great Western Railway Company purchased the canal and all its assets. As a result it gradually became derelict and eventually unnavigable. The National Trust took up a lease on the canal and, following a huge restoration programme, it was finally re-opened by British Waterways in 1964.

Cross the bridge and proceed right along the tow path towards Henley-in-Arden, taking time to appreciate the fine, old cast-iron split bridges which were built in two halves with a gap to allow through a towing rope pulled by the horses. Rejoin Walk 18 at the next lock gate by the A4189 (near Point ❹).

Brueton Park and the Grand Union Canal

DISTANCE 7 miles (11.3km)	MINIMUM TIME 3hrs

ASCENT/GRADIENT 33ft (10m) ▲▲▲   LEVEL OF DIFFICULTY ✦✦✦

PATHS Field footpaths and tow paths

LANDSCAPE Parkland, canalside and residential areas

SUGGESTED MAP OS Explorer 220 Birmingham

START/FINISH Grid reference: SP 162789

DOG FRIENDLINESS Off lead along tow path, otherwise under control

PARKING Brueton Park car park

PUBLIC TOILETS In Brueton Park

This enjoyable circuit starts in Brueton Park and encompasses a stroll along the Grand Union Canal, before finishing in Malvern Park. Brueton Park was gifted to Solihull in 1944 by the prominent local businessman and councillor Horace Brueton. It was formerly attached to Malvern Hall, and the two parks were linked in 1963. Today the two distinct parks form one large park to the southeast of Solihull town centre. The narrow strip of land follows a roughly U-shaped layout and covers an area of approximately 130 acres (53ha).

BRUETON PARK

Brueton Park incorporates a local nature reserve, and many species of mature trees including oak, ash and conifers can be found. Brueton Park Lake, which was formed by damming the local River Blythe, can be found at its southern end. Wildlife enthusiasts will find much of interest, with abundant birdlife on and surrounding the lake. The Parkridge Nature Centre in the middle of the park was opened in 2002 by the Warwickshire Wildlife Trust, when the park also received Local Nature Reserve status in recognition for its importance to wildlife. Here you will find an interesting conservation interpretation and education centre which provides workshops, talks and demonstrations, as well as a restaurant.

MALVERN PARK

By contrast, Malvern Park is a formal municipal town centre park, and throughout the year the floral displays are magnificent. It was originally laid out by the Urban District Council in 1926 on land partly forming a section of the estate of Malvern Hall and partly purchased from local farmers (Malvern Park Farm). The buildings of Malvern Hall, dating from about 1690 and a favourite subject for the painter John Constable, are now home to St Martin's Independent School for Girls.

A STATUESQUE GIFT

Malvern Park Avenue is dominated by a magnificent statue, the Prancing Horse and Man. It was the work of Vienna-born Joseph Edgar Boehm in 1874, and is thought to depict Alexander the Great and his famous horse Bucephalas. It was purchased at auction by Captain Oliver Bird, of Bird's Custard fame, for his garden in Solihull, but he donated it to the Solihull Council in 1945 and it was placed in Malvern Park in 1953, the Coronation year.

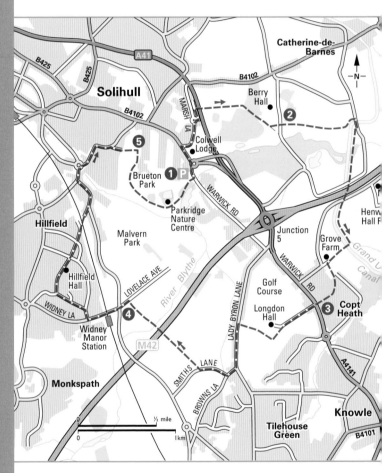

❶ Leave Brueton Park via exit the driveway. Go left through a cul-de-sac, then cross the B4025. Follow the pathway into Marsh Lane and continue to a roundabout. Turn right into Avenbury Drive. Go right through kissing gate before No. 16. Cross the A41 then go through a kissing gate and take the path on the right of a hedge, via a kissing gate. Follow the path over several fields, then go right

through a kissing gate into woodland. Follow a path via a kissing gate. Pass farm buildings and leave via three kissing gates. Continue across a paddock via two kissing gates and cross Ravenshaw Lane.

❷ Continue ahead through a kissing gate, walking to the right of a hedge over fields. Go through two further kissing gates, then left through a kissing gate onto a track leading to the canal. Cross a bridge to descend to tow path. Go left beneath the M42 and Barston Lane. Exit at bridge No. 75, via a stile. Cross a bridge and stile onto a footpath towards Grove Farm. Past the farm, go through a kissing gate and along a driveway. Go left over two stiles, and follow a footpath and lanes, skirting Knowle. Through a handgate, the footpath crosses a cul-de-sac onto a path beyond No. 15. At Keepers Cottage, bear right on the lane towards Warwick Road.

❸ Cross the road and follow the footpath towards Longdon Hall. Turn right at a junction, following the hedge towards the golf course. Cross this to reach a kissing gate into Lady Byron Lane. Go left, then right into Browns Lane and right into Smiths Lane. After about 325yds (297m) go right over a stile and footbridge into a garden, then over a stile into farmland. Keep to the right of two fields via a stile, then cross a footbridge over the M42 via two stiles. Continue ahead over a stile and footbridge over the River Blythe. Cross

another stile and follow a fenced footpath to the right of a field, then go over stile onto Lovelace Avenue.

❹ Turn left, crossing Widney Manor Road into Widney Lane. Go beneath a railway bridge, turn right into Alderminster Road then left into Libbards Way. Turn right into Fielding Lane and join Solihull Way. Pass Hillfield Hall, cross Alderminster Road and continue ahead on Fielding Lane, which becomes a walking/cycling route. Go beneath the railway bridge towards Church Hill Road. Bear left, then right up the path beside No. 57. At the end of the path turn right, rejoining Church Hill Road. Pass St Alphege's Church and school.

❺ Turn right to enter Malvern Park on a path between Malvern and Cedarhurst. Turn right before reaching ornate gate piers, passing to the right of tennis courts, then bear left into Malvern Park and follow a tarmac footpath until you come to Parkridge Nature Centre. Pass to the right to reach Brueton Park Lake, then turn left and walk along the lakeside to return to the car park.

WHERE TO EAT AND DRINK Opposite St Alphege's Church is The Masons Arms pub, which welcomes walkers. Supervised children are allowed in the bar. There are also many other options in the pedestrianised town centre of Solihull.

• • • •

WHAT TO SEE The Grand Union Canal, completed in 1805, forms the major part of a London–Birmingham link. The canal is managed by British Waterways, a state-owned public corporation. In recent years it has invested millions in maintaining and bringing the ageing canal network into the 21st century.

• • • •

WHILE YOU'RE THERE Solihull's High Street still contains some features of Tudor England. St Alphege's Church has a rare altar stone in the crypt and a brass portrait of William Hill (1549), along with his two wives, Isabel and Agnes, and three groups of 18 children.

Between the Lakes at Kingsbury Water Park

DISTANCE 3 miles (4.8km)	MINIMUM TIME 1hr 20min	

ASCENT/GRADIENT 33ft (10m) ▲▲▲   LEVEL OF DIFFICULTY ✦✦✦

PATHS Lakeside paths and footpaths

LANDSCAPE Lakes and parkland

SUGGESTED MAP OS Explorer 232 Nuneaton & Tamworth

START/FINISH Grid reference: SP 217962

DOG FRIENDLINESS Under control at all times

PARKING Pear Tree Avenue car park

PUBLIC TOILETS Visitor centre in Kingsbury Water Park

The water park around Kingsbury was once 620 acres (251ha) of old sand and gravel pits, but today it has become a major leisure facility with more than 30 beautiful lakes and pools attracting some 200,000 visitors each year.

WATER WONDERLAND

A path crosses the River Tame into the water park, where you can stroll around a number of the larger pools to enjoy the sight of a wide variety of contemporary sporting activities taking place such as sailing, windsurfing, fishing and horse-riding.

The old village of Kingsbury sits on a small hill overlooking this wonderland of water. On this high ground is the Church of St Peter and St Paul from where you get a delightful view over the lakes. The church has a 12th-century nave, a 14th-century tower and a 16th-century belfry. One of its old arches is incised by deep grooves in which it is believed local bowmen used to sharpen their arrows.

Kingsbury village has been associated with many famous families over the years. In the Middle Ages the Bracebridge and Arden families were involved in a Romeo-and-Juliet-type feud when Alice Bracebridge married John Arden against the wishes of both families. John's brother's granddaughter was Mary Arden, the mother of William Shakespeare.

LAND OF PEEL

By the middle of the 19th century most of the land in the village was owned by Sir Robert Peel. The long-serving MP for Tamworth, one-time Prime Minister and founder of the modern police, lived at nearby Drayton Manor and was buried at Drayton Basset, a few miles up the Tame Valley. The main business of the area had been agriculture, but coal mining took over. Later sand and gravel was extracted from the land on the other side of the River Tame. Today the river divides a thriving village from the Kingsbury Water Park.

HUNDREDS IN FLOOD

You leave the water park over Hemlingford Bridge, which crosses the River Tame. This bridge was first built by public subscription in 1783 and takes its name from the Hundred of Hemlingford in which Kingsbury stands (a hundred was an old Saxon local administrative area). There used to be a toll house at one end of the original bridge, but this was demolished in 1937. On New Year's Day in 1982 the original bridge was destroyed by catastrophic floods which swept down the Tame Valley. Flooding has been a regular feature of the area, with the water frequently rising and spreading over the flood plain between Kingsbury village and the nearby hamlet of Bodymoor Heath. Most people now choose to live on the east side of the River Tame.

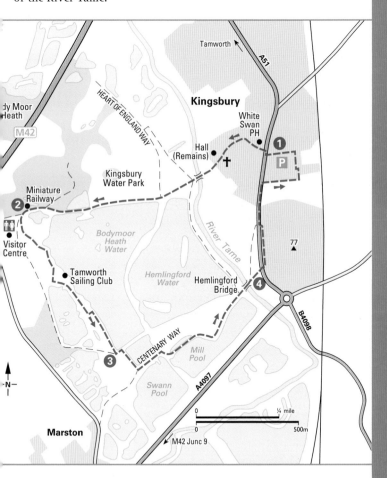

❶ From the car park, go left along Pear Tree Avenue to reach the A51 road. Go right along the pavement of the A51, then cross the road passing in front of the White Swan pub. About 35yds (32m) beyond the pub, cross over the road and go left along the well-walked footpath by the side of the churchyard. Follow the Heart of England waymarkers

Overleaf: Bodymoor Heath Water, Kingsbury Water Park (Walk 21)

past the church building and descend the steps to reach a footbridge over the River Tame. Cross the bridge and walk ahead along the gravel track to enter Kingsbury Water Park. With Hemlingford Water close on your left, cross the footbridge and walk by the side of Bodymoor Heath Water, leaving the Heart of England behind as you proceed ahead. Eventually bear left by the miniature railway and keep straight ahead past a children's play area to reach the visitor centre.

2 From the visitor centre, follow the signs to the watersports clubs along lanes and footpaths. Shortly the path returns to the side of Bodymoor Heath Water, then leaves it to pass by the entrance gate to Tamworth Sailing Club. Continue to the right-hand side of Bodymoor Heath Water, along a tarmac lane, then back to the water's edge path.

3 At the end of the stretch of Bodymoor Heath Water bear left, then almost immediately right and follow the waymarkers for the Centenary Way. Turning left, the waymarkers take you near to Swann Pool and then diagonally across a small car park, between Mill Pool and Hemlingford Water, as your route veers in a northeast direction. Continue on the path until it merges with a lane, then keep ahead to cross the Hemlingford Bridge.

4 On the far side of the bridge continue ahead up the lane to the main road. Cross over and turn left along the pavement towards Kingsbury. After 440yds(402m) reach an area of open land on the right. At the far end turn right, through a kissing gate, to the right of No. 61, onto a clear footpath that goes along the back of some houses. In about 220yds (201m) turn left into Meadow Close, then left again into Pear Tree Avenue to return to the car park.

WHERE TO EAT AND DRINK The White Swan, which you pass on your way into Kingsbury Water Park, is a regular haunt of local rambling groups. Well-behaved children and dogs are allowed in the bar. Alternatively you might like to try the Old Barn Coffee Shop at the visitor centre in the park. There is an outside seating area and a menu big enough to satisfy even the heartiest of appetites.

● ● ● ●

WHAT TO SEE Many wild birds visit the water park and you will certainly see plenty of ducks, swans, coots and moorhens, and especially Canada geese. Look out for herons, kingfishers, common terns, great crested grebes, cormorants, little ringed plovers and lapwings. Some 200 species of bird have been recorded here, and the park has one of the UK's largest inland breeding colonies of common terns.

● ● ● ●

WHILE YOU'RE THERE Kingsbury's Norman church stands on a hill overlooking the River Tame where the kings of Mercia were said to have had a palace. Mercia was the main Saxon kingdom at the time of King Offa, who died in AD 796. Close to the church, the crumbling wall round Kingsbury Hall is now part of a farmhouse, which retains its Elizabethan splendour.

By Baddesley Clinton

DISTANCE 5 miles (8km)   MINIMUM TIME 2hrs

ASCENT/GRADIENT 16ft (5m) ▲▲▲   LEVEL OF DIFFICULTY ✦✦✦

PATHS Field paths and woodland tracks

LANDSCAPE Rolling Warwickshire countryside

SUGGESTED MAP OS Explorer 221 Coventry & Warwick

START/FINISH Grid reference: SP 206706

DOG FRIENDLINESS On lead at all times

PARKING Lay-by beside Hay Wood picnic area, Hay Wood Lane

PUBLIC TOILETS None on route

This lovely walk through the heart of Warwickshire's delightful countryside provides the opportunity to visit Baddesley Clinton Manor. This historic mansion is one of the finest medieval moated manor houses in the country.

NO CHANGE AT THE MANOR

Baddesley Clinton Manor is the former home of the Ferrers, family and its wide moat may date back to Norman times. The bridge that spans the moat is comparatively recent, being only 200 or so years old. Many of the Ferrers family were laid to rest in the nearby church. Sir Edward Ferrers, the first of some 12 generations, died in 1535.

Henry Ferrers, who was born in 1549, was probably the most famous member of the family. Many people enjoyed his verse in the time of Elizabeth I and he became a notable antiquarian. The Ferrers family, staunchly loyal to the Roman Catholic faith, were persecuted throughout the 16th century by the Protestant authorities. When Henry Ferrers let the house out in the 1590s it became a regular refuge for Jesuit priests. On one occasion as many as six were hidden in specially built priest holes, which can still be seen around the house today. The family fell on hard times again during the Civil War, when they were made to pay for their support for Charles I.

Despite a few embellishments over the years, the house has seen little real change since Henry's death in 1633. It stayed in the Ferrers family until 1940, and is now owned and managed by the National Trust.

WREN'S ABBEY

Nearby Wroxall Abbey was founded by Benedictine nuns in 1135. Owned and occupied by the Bourgoyne family for many years, it was purchased by the architect Sir Christopher Wren as a retreat just three years after he completed his work on St Paul's Cathedral, in London in 1710. Sadly his house was replaced by the current heavy Victorian one in the 1860s. Today only St Leonard's Church and part of the cloisters remain, surrounded by glorious gardens.

HEART OF ENGLAND WAY

You start the walk by crossing Hay Wood. After following tracks and quiet lanes, the route brings you back through the splendid park of Wroxall Abbey. From here you continue past a converted windmill on the edge of the village of Rowington Green and join the Heart of England Way long distance footpath. Fine Warwickshire countryside and footpaths, lined with flowers in the spring, then lead to the church close to Baddesley Clinton Manor.

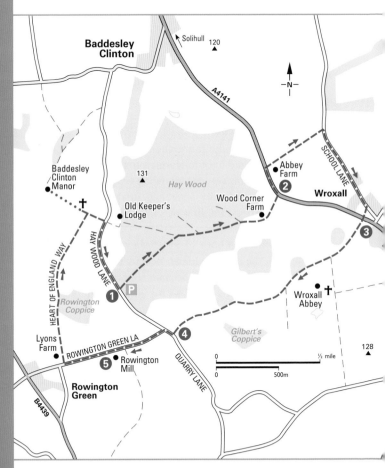

1 From the picnic area lay-by, take the metalled track into Hay Wood. At a crossing of paths, go right along the bridleway. Nearing the edge of the woods, the clear path arcs left and you emerge from the trees via a handgate. Cross the field to a gate

and pass between the buildings to a double gate. Through these go left then right by Wood Corner Farm, and along the drive to reach the A4141.

2 Cross the road and go left along the pavement of the A4141 for about

220yds (201m), then go right along a bridleway between the buildings of Abbey Farm. Continue along the track until you reach School Lane and walk right along it towards the A4141. About 100yds (91m) before you reach the end of the lane, go right through a handgate and cross the corner of a field to reach the A4141 via a kissing gate near the Ducklings Day Nursery.

3 Cross the A4141, enter Wroxall Abbey park over a stile and through a field gate, then follow the track through the grounds. In about 500yds (457m) the route gives you glimpses of the Victorian mansion and the old abbey building, which you can see to your left. Where the track peters out continue ahead through two kissing gates and then bear half left towards a kissing gate set in a small area of enclosed woodland. Exit from the woodland via a kissing gate. Follow this path ahead as it descends in a southwesterly direction to a waymark post. Continue ahead to go through another kissing gate and a field gate.

Head west-southwest across a large area of pasture, passing to the right of Gilbert's Coppice and a solitary pollarded oak. Through a kissing gate, bear right along the field edge to a field gate onto Quarry Lane.

4 Turn right along the lane, then bear left at the junction and walk along the quiet Rowington Green Lane for almost 0.5 miles (800m).

5 Pass by the former windmill on the left, and just before reaching Lyons Farm, go right through a field gate onto a track which is part of the Heart of England Way. The route takes you to the right of the farm complex, via a gate, and then along a track which bears right. After passing Rowington Coppice you come to a handgate. Through this, continue ahead on field paths alongside hedges, crossing the corner of a field via two handgates and a footbridge. Reaching the church driveway, turn right and then right again to walk along Hay Wood Lane, back to the parking area.

WHERE TO EAT AND DRINK There are no pubs along the route but you will find refreshment at The Barn Restaurant and tea rooms at Baddesley Clinton Manor. Here you can indulge in a fine selection of home-cooked foods from soup and a roll to tasty turkey in orange. The apple and orange tart is particularly sublime.

••••

WHAT TO SEE Hay Wood was once part of the ancient Forest of Arden and later owned by Baddesley Clinton Estate. Today it is commercially managed by the Forestry Commission. They have retained a mix of woodland and you'll see the track is lined with oak, rowan, birch and holly.

••••

WHILE YOU'RE THERE The National Trust's Packwood House stands in hidden countryside less than 3 miles (4.8km) from Baddesley Clinton Manor. The building was created by Graham Baron Ash and contains fine collections of 16th-century textiles and furniture. It is most famous for its exceptional collection of 17th-century yew trees said to represent the Sermon on the Mount.

A Tour of Historic Stratford-upon-Avon

DISTANCE 2.5 miles (4km)	MINIMUM TIME 1hr 30min

ASCENT/GRADIENT Negligible ▲▲▲   LEVEL OF DIFFICULTY ✦✦✦

PATHS Riverside paths and street pavements

LANDSCAPE Historic streets

SUGGESTED MAP OS Explorer 205 Stratford-upon-Avon & Evesham

START/FINISH Grid reference: SP 205547

DOG FRIENDLINESS On lead along streets

PARKING Recreation Ground pay-and-display car park

PUBLIC TOILETS At car park and top of Henley Street

This gentle walk along the banks of the River Avon takes you past the weir and Holy Trinity Church, before a stroll through the town to see some of the famous buildings in Shakespeare's Stratford.

The medieval 14-arched Clopton Bridge forms a splendid gateway to the town. The Town Hall is a fine Palladian building, and Harvard House in the High Street dates from 1596. The latter takes its name from the owner's daughter, Katherine Rogers, who married Robert Harvard of Southwark in London in 1605. Their son John went on to bequeath Harvard University in the USA, and the university now owns Harvard House. The Falcon Hotel was probably one of Shakespeare's regular drinking places and opposite is the ancient guildhall and an attractive row of timbered almshouses.

THE MAIN ATTRACTION

But it is because of William Shakespeare that visitors flock in their millions to Stratford-upon-Avon. Born here, in Henley Street, in 1564, he was baptised in Holy Trinity Church, and attended King Edward VI's Grammar School in Church Street. He married Anne Hathaway in 1582 and they had three children: Susannah, Hamnet and Judith. However, a country market town was no place for a playwright and poet, so some time in the mid-1580s he headed for London.

By 1592 William Shakespeare was the talk of the town, counting Queen Elizabeth and her court among his plays' many admirers. His poetry was first published around this time, and he began to accumulate serious wealth. By 1597 he was able to buy New Place, then one of Stratford's grandest properties. The early 1600s saw his theatre company gain a royal title (the King's Men), and the Bard went on to write many of his best-known tragedies, including *Othello, King Lear* and *Macbeth*.

Shakespeare began to spend less and less time in the giddy London theatre-world, and more time at home in Stratford. His son Hamnet had died, aged 11, in 1596, but the boy's sister Susannah had survived and married Dr John Hall in 1607. The couple lived in Hall's Croft, in the old part of the town, until after her father's death. Shakespeare died on 23 April 1616 and was buried at Holy Trinity. You can see his tomb, and that of his wife Anne Hathaway, who died in 1623. It bears the inscription:

'Good friend for Jesus sake forebeare
To dig the dust encloased heare!
Bleste be the man that spares the stones
And curst be he that moves the bones.'

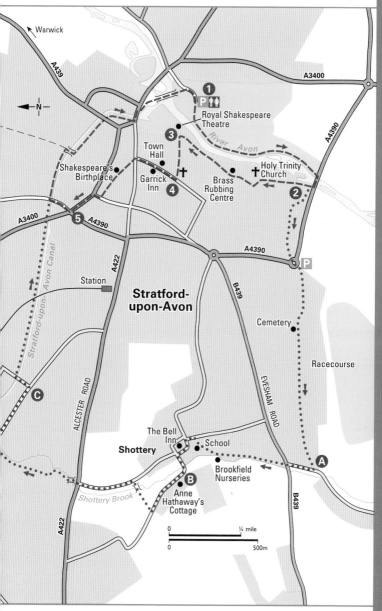

1 From the car park, walk along the banks of the River Avon opposite the famous Royal Shakespeare Theatre. Pass the weir, and continue to reach a footbridge over the river, just in front of the A4390 road bridge.

2 Go right over the footbridge and bear right past the flats that replaced the old watermill, into Mill Lane. Continue up Mill Lane and go through the churchyard of Holy Trinity Church, walking around the church to see the river view. Leave the churchyard through the main gate into Old Town and follow the pavement. Just before reaching the turn into Southern Lane, go right into RSC Gardens and walk up to the Brass Rubbing Centre. Continue past the ferry and stroll through the attractive Theatre Gardens by the side of the Avon, exiting into Waterside and passing by the frontage of the old theatre building.

3 Go left up Chapel Lane. At the top of the lane is the Guild Chapel to Shakespeare's Grammar School, with New Place Gardens to the right.

4 Go right along Chapel Street, passing The Shakespeare and the Town Hall into High Street. Harvard House is on the left, near the black-and-white Garrick Inn. At the end of High Street, bear left around the traffic island into Henley Street and walk along the pedestrianised area that takes you past Shakespeare's Birthplace and the museum. At the top of Henley Street, bear right and then left into Birmingham Road. Go left up to the traffic lights and cross the road at the pedestrian crossing.

5 Head right up Clopton Road for 100yds (91m), then descend to the tow path of the Stratford-upon-Avon Canal at bridge No. 66. Follow this, going southeast. Cross the canal at bridge No. 68 and continue along the tow path into Bancroft Gardens by the canal basin, where you will see an array of narrowboats and the Royal Shakespeare Theatre. Cross the old Tram Bridge to return to the car park on the right.

WHERE TO EAT AND DRINK This short route passes The Black Swan pub in Southern Lane (known locally as 'The Dirty Duck') which is frequented by actors from the theatre. The half-timbered Garrick Inn in High Street is popular with the local rugby club. The Bell in nearby Shottery has long been used by local walking groups.

● ● ● ●

WHAT TO SEE Back in the 1970s and 1980s, the swans virtually disappeared from the River Avon due to poisoning by lead fishing weights. Today they have returned, and together with ducks add considerable interest to the many photo opportunities available. In the canal basin, narrow boats assemble to form a colourful foreground for photographs of the Gower Memorial, which depicts Shakespeare and characters from the Bard's famous plays.

● ● ● ●

WHILE YOU'RE THERE Spare time to visit some of the fantastic Shakespeare properties and indulge in the wonderful medieval atmosphere that permeates this beautiful town.

From Stratford to Anne Hathaway's Cottage

DISTANCE 5.5 miles (8.8km)   MINIMUM TIME 2hrs 30min

ASCENT/GRADIENT Negligible ▲▲▲   LEVEL OF DIFFICULTY +++

SEE MAP AND INFORMATION PANEL FOR WALK 23

Once over the footbridge at Point ②, walk ahead up the tarmac footpath away from the river that follows the line of the A4390, then arcs right and then left. Cross over Meadowbank Road (by Avon Meadow Close), and after a short stretch of path continue through Old Town Mews, an estate road, to the roundabout on the A4390. By its side, cross the road with care, then proceed along the pavement into residential Wetherby Way. Follow the tarmac path to the right of No. 2, soon passing the cemetery hedge, and continue on a footpath through common land at the back of houses. This follows the track bed of a former railway line. At the end of the common you will come to the Luddington Road, with Stratford Racecourse entrance to the left (Point Ⓐ).

Go sharp right along Luddington Road up to the B439 Evesham road. Cross and walk along the signed footpath opposite, by the side of Shottery Brook. Footpaths and a pavement will take you along Hogarth Road, then follow another footpath to the driveway to Brookfield Nurseries. Go right up the driveway into Shottery. At the main road, go left past Shottery St Andrew Primary School

and The Bell, then left down Cottage Lane and walk up to the picturesque Anne Hathaway's Cottage (Point Ⓑ). Continue past the cottage and in about 300yds (274m), go right on a tarmac footpath, passing several thatched cottages. You will emerge on the pavement in Church Lane, where you go left up to the A422 Alcester Road.

Cross the A422 and continue up a footpath opposite, to the right of Bridge House, which meanders along the side of Shottery Brook. At the end of a grassed area, bear left and go up to a residential road. Go right, then left to join a footpath alongside the Shottery Brook. Cross a road and continue ahead, to follow the left bank of the brook for 120yds (110m). Go right over a footbridge behind some swings onto the pavement of a road of industrial buildings. Follow the pavement alongside the road for some 350yds (320m), then turn left into Timothy Bridge Road (Point Ⓒ). Cross the canal bridge and descend right to the tow path which leads back into Stratford-upon-Avon. You will pass by a number of moored narrowboats and rejoin Walk 23 by the Clopton road bridge, No. 65 (Point ⑤).

On the Centenary Way from Ilmington

DISTANCE 3 miles (4.8km)	MINIMUM TIME 1hr 30min

ASCENT/GRADIENT 492ft (150m) ▲▲▲　　LEVEL OF DIFFICULTY ✦✦✦

PATHS Field paths and country lane

LANDSCAPE Edge of Cotswold Hills

SUGGESTED MAP OS Explorer 205 Stratford-upon-Avon & Evesham

START/FINISH Grid reference: SP 210440

DOG FRIENDLINESS On lead at all times

PARKING Playing fields car park, on Mickleton Road west of Ilmington village

PUBLIC TOILETS None on route

Remote Ilmington is the highest village in Warwickshire, standing close to the borders of Worcestershire and Gloucestershire, and just within the Cotswolds Area of Outstanding Natural Beauty. Brimming with typical Cotswold honey-coloured stone cottages, it is a place where time seems to have stood still for centuries. The name is probably derived from a Saxon phrase describing elms on a border hill. A mid-10th century record reveals its earlier name was Ylmandunes.

ROYAL GUEST

In 1934 Ilmington achieved a brief five minutes of fame when part of the very first Christmas broadcast by King George V was relayed to the Empire from Ilmington Manor, the home of the Flower family. It featured a guest appearance by local shepherd, 65-year-old Walter Walton Handy, and also included carols from the Ilmington Singers and bell ringing from the village. The local papers were delighted with the story, describing it as 'perhaps the most wonderful (feat) that has been accomplished since wireless has been brought to its present state of perfection'.

As in many small country villages today, local facilities are fast disappearing. Although Ilmington Village Hall plays host to an 'outreach' post office and there is still a small village primary school, it no longer has a general shop. However, it has managed to retain its two pubs – The Red Lion and The Howard Arms – and these are enthusiastically supported by local walkers. The Ilmington Morris Dancers, carrying on a tradition that has been practised in the village for 350 years, are well known and can be seen performing regularly in the area on summer evenings.

THE CHURCH MICE

This walk, hilly by Warwickshire standards, starts from the edge of the village. Climbing to a high point of almost 200m near Upper

Lark Stoke Farm, it offers some of the best views in the county. Having crossed farmland and strolled along a quiet country lane, walkers will spot the Norman church, with its fine tower, among the trees as the route drops back towards the village. The church itself is well worth a visit. It has oak pews installed in the 1930s, which feature the unique carved mouse 'signature' of master craftsman Robert Thompson, known as the Mouseman of Kilburn. The 17th-century gabled manor house can also be seen.

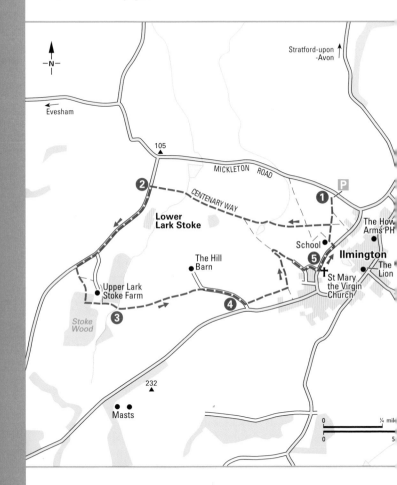

❶ Cross the playing fields to go through a kissing gate to the right of a children's play area. Bear right and go through another kissing gate. Bear right again, aiming for a kissing gate in the hedge on the far side of the field. Continue in the same direction, crossing several fields. After two more kissing gates, bear left through another one, hidden from view at first. Walk gently uphill beside a hedge and then through a kissing gate, continuing in the same direction beside a fence on the right. There are fine Cotswold hill views, with an attractive farmhouse at Lower Lark Stoke ahead. Descend to go through a gate near a small pool, and bear left to walk beside the fence. Go through a gate to emerge on a driveway, along which you turn right.

2 Turn left along a tarmac lane and follow this uphill for about 0.5 miles (800m), stopping occasionally to recover your breath and to enjoy wonderful retrospective views. After the farm drive and just before the brow of the hill, go left across a field. Entering an area of young woodland just above Upper Lark Stoke Farm, keep right at a path fork. Go left just before a gate within more mature woodland, and then descend into a dell. Go through a gate, and continue downhill in the same direction to cross a small stream.

3 Bear left, uphill, to cross a footbridge and go through a gate. Keep straight ahead to climb towards the hilltop, passing to the right of a solitary tree. Over the brow, descend to a field gate. Walk beside the fence on the right and through another field gate to join a farm track. After passing the grassed-over drive to The Hill

Barn, over to the left, the track bends sharp right.

4 Just before reaching a road, cross a stile next to a gate on the left. Walk with the hedge on your left, descending towards Ilmington. At the bottom of the slope, go left over a stile in the trees, then right alongside a hedge. This path leads to a gate and stile, after which you turn right to follow a hedged track that leads to some buildings. Turn left, through two gates in quick succession, and then double back right, along Ilmington Grange's tarmac drive.

5 Go left at the road and then, immediately after the entrance to Ilmington Primary School, turn left through a kissing gate. Go through the gate on the right and cross the field to a kissing gate. Retracing your steps, bear left through another kissing gate and back across the playing fields to the car park.

WHERE TO EAT AND DRINK The Red Lion is a favourite eating place with local walkers, and reasonably priced food is the order of the day – try the excellent home-made soup. Children and dogs are allowed in the pub, and there is also a small rear garden. The Howard Arms, once owned by the Howard family from the nearby hamlet of Foxcote, enjoys a peaceful setting on the village green and offers delicious food and a quiet pint.

● ● ● ●

WHAT TO SEE Crab Mill is a lovely old building, built from local stone. Early in the 20th century it was home to Lady Borwick, whose fortune came from baking powder. Later it was occupied by Dorothy Crowfoot Hodgkin, who won a Nobel Prize for Chemistry in 1964 for her pioneering work in crystallography.

● ● ● ●

WHILE YOU'RE THERE Nearby Chipping Campden, 5 miles (8km) southwest of Ilmington, is a typical wool town built by the affluent merchants of the 14th and 15th centuries. It has many gabled Cotswold stone houses with oriel, dormer and mullioned windows, and an outstanding market hall. A visit to this wonderful old market town is almost like taking a step back into the Middle Ages.

From Shustoke to Church End

DISTANCE 4 miles (6.4km)	MINIMUM TIME 1hr 45min	
ASCENT/GRADIENT 98ft (30m) ▲▲▲	LEVEL OF DIFFICULTY ✦✦✦	

PATHS Lakeside paths and field-edge footpaths

LANDSCAPE Reservoir parkland, farmland and residential areas

SUGGESTED MAP OS Explorer 232 Nuneaton & Tamworth

START/FINISH Grid reference: SP 225909

DOG FRIENDLINESS Under control at all times

PARKING Severn Trent car park, Shustoke

PUBLIC TOILETS None on route

The beautiful Shustoke Reservoir, together with nearby Whitacre Water Works, supplies water to the bulk storage reservoirs at Coventry and Nuneaton. The reservoir is a well-used sailing venue, and is also popular with anglers and walkers.

The small village of Shustoke, from which the reservoir takes its name, lies on the edge of Warwickshire. It was once a large parish, covering some 2,000 acres (810ha), but much of this is now under water. The village was mentioned in the Domesday survey as Scotscote, but has gone through a series of name changes over the centuries including Schustoke, Sydestoke, Shestoke, Schristoke, Sheistock and Shstooke. Its origins perhaps lie in the Saxon 'sceat' meaning 'nook' or 'corner of land'. Shustoke is a divided village because of an outbreak of the plague in 1650. It used to surround St Cuthbert's Church, but the houses were moved to the west to get away from the contaminated site.

DUGDALE THE ANTIQUARY

Shustoke's most famous son is Sir William Dugdale (1605–86), the author of *The Antiquities of Warwickshire*. He was born at the old rectory in Shawbury Lane, the son of a Lancashire gentleman who settled in Warwickshire after marrying late in life. Today a large part of the local land is still owned by the Dugdale family.

William Dugdale was schooled at Coventry, and came back to live at Blyth Hill in Shustoke after his marriage in 1625. He was one of a group of local gentry who took up the study of local history, and it was through this that he came into contact with members of the court of Charles I. He secured a post at the College of Arms, and spent most of the Civil War in the Royalist stronghold of Oxford, where he was able to pursue his studies in the Bodleian Library. As well as Warwickshire, he focused his attention on English monastic houses. The first volume of his *Monasticon Anglicanum* was published in 1655, with two more huge volumes following in

1661 and 1673. *The Antiquities of Warwickshire*, the most detailed study of its day, was published in 1655. He also wrote a *History of St Paul's Cathedral*, published in 1658.

The Restoration was kind to Dugdale and he was able to continue with his heraldic work all over the country. He was appointed Garter King of Arms in 1677 and died, aged 80, in 1686. He was buried in the village.

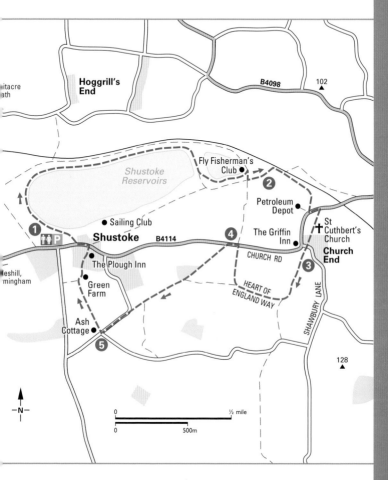

❶ Leave the car park going up to the reservoir embankment and go left to follow the fingerpost of the Circular Path, which encircles the larger of the two Shustoke reservoirs. At the east end of the reservoir, go through a gate and immediately left down steps, then go right along a metalled track. Meeting a tarmac lane, go left over a footbridge, then along a path parallel to the lane which is a short distance to the south of the smaller reservoir – this is to protect you from the possible danger of fly fishing lines. After passing behind the buildings of the Fly Fisherman's Club, leave the reservoir complex over a stile and go right along a path in woodland and cross a footbridge.

❷ Emerge from the trees via a gate and turn left. Follow the field edge to a further gate and continue along a field edge, the railway on your left, before curving up to the B4114 at the entrance to a petroleum depot. Turn left along the road edge for 80yds (73m), then cross the road and go through a kissing gate into the pasture below St Cuthbert's Church. Walk half right up the field and go through a second kissing gate to the right-hand side of the churchyard, and take the lane past the church to Shawbury Lane.

3 Cross the lane and go through a kissing gate, situated a little to the right, into the field opposite. Following the direction of the waymarkers across two fields, via a gate and a kissing gate, to meet the Heart of England Way. Do not go through the kissing gate, but go right to a kissing gate in the field corner and follow the Way around the next two fields. Bear right at the end of the larger field to walk up to Church Road, via three kissing gates. Go left along the road for 50yds (46m).

4 At the end of a small row of cottages, turn left through a handgate, and cross the field half right to a kissing gate. Take the public footpath through a small copse and then continue ahead by the side of the hedge until, via a kissing gate, you come to a farm track that leads to the corner of a lane. Through another kissing gate, continue ahead along the lane.

5 Just before you reach Ash Cottage, go right through a kissing gate and follow the footpath across a cultivated field to a kissing gate to the left of Green Farm. A final kissing gate to the right of Greenacre (cottage) leads into a lane. Continue ahead and you soon reach the Green in Shustoke, close to The Plough Inn and at the side of the B4114 (Coleshill Road). Go left, then right into the Severn Trent car park.

WHERE TO EAT AND DRINK The Plough Inn, by the Green, offers traditional ales, quality meals, and bed and breakfast. It's popular with rambling groups and families (dogs allowed in the bar only). The Griffin Inn at Church End has a good selection of bar snacks and serves Vicars Ruin ale. Children are welcome in the conservatory, dogs are allowed in the bar area.

● ● ● ●

WHAT TO SEE Shustoke attracts a wide range of birdlife to its valuable open water. As well as pochard, teal, widgeon and tufted duck, the occasional osprey has been sighted, dipping this way on its passage south in November. You may also spy the distinctive profile of a cormorant, patiently fishing at the water's edge.

● ● ● ●

WHILE YOU'RE THERE Not far away from Shustoke is Hoar Park Farm, an 18th-century farm complex which has been converted to accommodate a lively craft village and children's farm. There is also a country shopping area, an antiques centre, a garden centre and a restaurant, open all year round from Tuesday to Sunday.

A Circuit from Beautiful Berkswell

DISTANCE 5 miles (8km)	MINIMUM TIME 2hrs

ASCENT/GRADIENT 115ft (35m) ▲▲▲   LEVEL OF DIFFICULTY ✚✚✚

PATHS Field paths and parkland footpaths

LANDSCAPE Gentle, rolling farmland and parkland

SUGGESTED MAP OS Explorer 221 Coventry & Warwick

START/FINISH Grid reference: SP 244791

DOG FRIENDLINESS Off lead through Sixteen Acre Wood, otherwise under strict control

PARKING Free car park near church in Berkswell

PUBLIC TOILETS None on route

There are few nicer places to visit in Warwickshire than Berkswell, with its red-roofed, white-timbered cottages, the beautiful church, intriguing five-holed stocks and two historic pubs.

ANCIENT WELL TOWN

The old Saxon village was mentioned in the Domesday Book and has been variously called Berchewelle, Berkeswelle, Bercleswelle and finally Berkswell. It is believed that the village took its name from the 16-ft (4.8m), square well that is situated behind the almshouses. The 12th-century Church of St John the Baptist displays a wonderful two-storeyed, gabled and timbered porch which dates from the 16th century. Inside this lovely building is an old crypt conceivably dating from Saxon times, some 800-year-old stone seats along the walls, a Russian flag which was brought home from the Crimean War and magnificent choir stalls decorated with poppy heads and the figures of three saints – Wulfstan, Dunstan and Chad.

Although the nearby five-holed stocks were probably originally built with six holes, it is more fun to believe the local legend that they were specially made to accommodate a one-legged man and his two drunken companions.

WAR LINKS

There is a 16th-century pub in the village – The Bear Inn. The Bear has often been described as 'the perfect example of the old English inn', and the fine half-timbered building was once part of the Berkswell Estate and carried the coat of arms of the Earls of Warwick. It has links dating to the Civil War – some of Cromwell's troops were stationed at Berkswell and would have undoubtedly rested and drunk here.

A 19th-century Russian cannon, which was captured during the Crimean War in 1855 by Captain Arthur Eardley-Wilmot, the lord of the manor, stands on the front terrace of the inn. It was last fired in 1897 to mark the Diamond Jubilee of Queen Victoria. Apparently several windows in the village were shattered by the noise.

BERKSWELL HALL

Set in beautiful farmland on the far side of the lake is Berkswell Hall, once the family home of the Eardley-Wilmots. John Eardley-Wilmot went to school with the English writer, biographer and critic Dr Samuel Johnson in the 1720s. The hall has now been converted into private residential apartments.

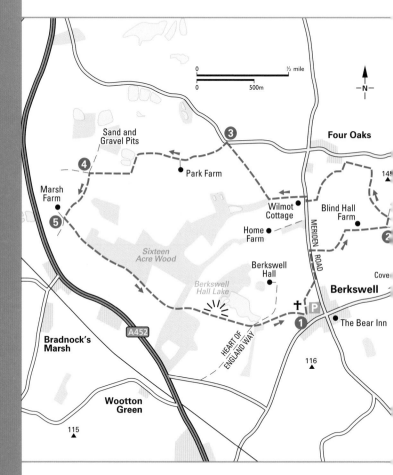

1 From the car park go right onto Church Lane and, just past the school but before the church in Berkswell, go right through a kissing gate. Follow the Heart of England Way to Meriden Road via four kissing gates. Go left along the road for 300yds (274m), having crossed to the pavement on the opposite side. Go right up a farm lane, passing through a kissing gate by a cattle grid and then Blind Hall Farm.

2 At the end of the lane/track go through a kissing gate by the farm gate, bear sharp left and walk along the field edge to its left corner, just past a small pond. Go left over a footbridge and then through a kissing gate and continue by the left-hand side of the hedge. The waymarked footpath weaves in and out of the hedge. After continuing ahead through a wide hedge gap, walk to the field corner and go left, skirting a small pond, to reach a kissing gate by some houses in Four Oaks. Ignore the kissing gate and bear left. In 90 paces go right over a plank footbridge and stile to cross the large, cultivated field diagonally, and exit onto Meriden Road via a kissing gate. Cross over and continue down the driveway to the right of Wilmot Cottage opposite, going through a gateway onto farmland. The path goes to the right of the hedge for two fields, crossing one stile, offering a clear view of Home Farm to the left; then, over another stile, crosses a third field diagonally. In about 625yds (571m), through a smaller field, you will reach the corner of Mercote Hall Lane via a kissing gate.

❸ Go left along the Mercote Hall Lane for about 0.5 miles (800m), passing the Park Farm complex. Pass through a wicket gate and walk along the lane past the large enclosed sand and gravel pits.

❹ At the end of the pit area, at a track junction, go left along a footpath to the left of a copse, then right over a footbridge and stile. Cross to a gate and footbridge, ascend to a kissing gate and walk to the left of a hedge on the approach to Marsh Farm.

❺ Just beyond the farm, turn left and follow the farm track alongside the hedge towards Sixteen Acre Wood. Cross the stile into the wood and take the track along the wood edge for some 700yds (640m). Emerging from the woodland, join the footpath for two fields, with the hedge on your left, then go through a strip of trees into former parkland via a kissing gate. Follow the path quarter-left across the cultivated field for some 650yds (594m) and you will enjoy a magnificent view of Berkswell Hall Lake. Enter trees and go left through a kissing gate to rejoin the Heart of England Way. Cross the footbridge onto a planked causeway with Berkswell Hall to your left. Continue ahead to a kissing gate. Go on through a tree belt to a kissing gate and then a gate, and back into Berkswell. Go through the churchyard to return to the car park.

WHERE TO EAT AND DRINK In Berkswell, The Bear Inn, near the junction of the Meriden and Coventry roads, has a large car park and good gardens. Children are allowed in this pub, but dogs are restricted to the large garden area. In the village also, near the church, is the friendly Berkswell Village Store and Tea Room.

● ● ● ●

WHAT TO SEE The Tsarist Russian flag in the Church of St John the Baptist displays a double-headed eagle. It was captured by Captain Eardley-Wilmot of Berkswell Hall during the Crimean War in 1855.

● ● ● ●

WHILE YOU'RE THERE Visit the beautiful Church of St John the Baptist in Berkswell. Can you spot woodcarver Robert Thompson's 'signature' (carved mice) in his woodwork? There are 17 of them.

Overleaf: The lake at Berkswell Hall (Walk 27)

A Loop from Long Hill to Ettington

DISTANCE 6 miles (9.7km)	MINIMUM TIME 2hrs

ASCENT/GRADIENT 345ft (105m) ▲▲▲   LEVEL OF DIFFICULTY ✦✦✦

PATHS Field paths, farm tracks and country lanes

LANDSCAPE Gentle, rolling countryside

SUGGESTED MAP OS Explorer 205 Stratford-upon-Avon & Evesham

START/FINISH Grid reference: SP 251518

DOG FRIENDLINESS On lead at all times

PARKING Large lay-by at Long Hill in Blue Lane

PUBLIC TOILETS None on route

Every road east of Stratford-upon-Avon appears to lead to Ettington, a small village that is bypassed by most people on their way to Banbury or Stratford. If you stop here, however, you will discover a lively place at the junction of two former turnpike roads.

Originally there were two villages – Upper Eatington and Lower Eatington, separated by a 1.5-mile (2.4km) gap. The Shirley family lived in the impressive high Victorian manor house in Lower Eatington for many years. At the end of the 18th century they decided to landscape their estate, with the result that the village disappeared leaving just their house and the church, which became the family chapel.

THREE CHURCHES

The family then gave land to Upper Eatington village and a new (second) church, the Church of St Thomas à Becket, was built in 1798. At roughly the same time Upper Eatington was renamed Ettington and the former Lower Eatington became part of the parish of Ettington.

The manor house is now the prestigious Ettington Park Hotel, but its chapel has become a ruin. Unfortunately the Church of St Thomas à Becket was built of poor quality materials and it quickly fell into disrepair. The tower, which has become part of a residential property and remains a local landmark at the entrance to Ettington village, is all that is left. In 1903, the Church of Holy Trinity and St Thomas of Canterbury was funded by public subscription.

A VERY ENGLISH SCENE

The walk starts from a lay-by on the Loxley Road, a mile (1.6km) or so out of the village, and follows a farm track towards Ettington. After passing the two Ettington churches it ascends into open countryside along a lovely stretch of footpath with fine views. The walk is completed with a stroll back up a quiet country lane.

1 From the lay-by at Long Hill, walk down the lane towards Loxley. In about 0.5 miles (800m) go right up the lane, past Hillside View and towards Ettingley Farm. Continue ahead to the right of Ettingley Farm, now a track. Through a field gate continue ahead across a field to a gate in the hedge. Descend across the next field, and at a path junction go ahead through a handgate to join the path to the right of the hedge, passing to the right of Whitfield Farm. Through a kissing gate, join the farm drive and follow it down to the A429.

2 Go right along the right-hand grass verge of the A429 towards Ettington, then in about 600yds (549m) cross the busy road with care and go left through a handgate in the hedge. Turn right and follow the path to left of the hedge to reach on to the old Warwick Road. Follow this traffic-free, disused road up to the A422 in the village, which brings you to a crossroads opposite the Church of Holy Trinity and St Thomas of Canterbury.

3 Go right along the A422 Banbury to Stratford-upon-Avon road, passing by the tower of St Thomas à Becket. Just before reaching the large roundabout, cross the road and follow the grass verge along the side of the A429 for 50 paces. Cross the A429, then climb the embankment opposite and go over a plank footbridge at the top and onto a farm drive. Go left along the drive, which leads to Grove Farm, taking time to enjoy the fine view to the right.

4 Walk between the buildings of Grove Farm, then bear right along the lane/track that passes to the left of woodland. Beyond the woodland end, the track bends left. Go through a kissing gate and pass to the left of Boundary Covert. Now the farm track becomes grass underfoot as you proceed along the ridge with extensive views all around. Go right at a junction of paths and continue to the left of the covert. Go down the track past the end of Nut Wood where it soon becomes a fenced footpath. Shortly come to the Alderminster road, near Goldicote Business Park. Cross the road, then the main A422 (take care here) and go left along the wide grass verge of the A429, past the business park entrance.

5 In about 500yds (457m) go right and walk up Blue Lane towards Loxley, passing by Blue Lane Farm on the way back to the lay-by and your car.

WHERE TO EAT AND DRINK There are two pubs along the A422 Banbury road in Ettington. The Chequers Inn is a bar/restaurant at the southeast end of the village. The 17th-century White Horse is near the end of Hockley Lane, and offers a selection of bar meals.

● ● ● ●

WHAT TO SEE Take a detour to see the ruins of the old church in Ettington Park, and note the epitaph to Anthony Underhill of 1587 in its tower. It ends:
'As dreams do slide, as bubbles rise and fall
As flowers do fade and flourish in an hour,
As smoke doth rise and vapours vanish all
Beyond the wilt or reach of human power,
As summer's heat doth parch the withered grass,
Such is our state, so life of man doth pass.'

● ● ● ●

WHILE YOU'RE THERE Honington Hall, 'the perfect English country house', lies 5 miles (8km) south of Ettington. Built in the 1680s for Sir Henry Parker, a wealthy London merchant, this magnificent manor house is set in 15 acres (6ha) of grounds. An octagonal saloon, said to be unique in England, was added in 1751.

Exploring the Ettington Countryside

DISTANCE 8.5 miles (13.7km)   **MINIMUM TIME** 3hrs 15min

ASCENT/GRADIENT 279ft (85m) ▲▲▲   **LEVEL OF DIFFICULTY** +++

SEE MAP AND INFORMATION PANEL FOR WALK 28

Leave Walk 28 at the A429 (Point ❷) and cross over the road with care, bearing right onto the driveway towards a farm complex, passing former railway station buildings, which closed in 1963. Bear left past some stables alongside a stream, going left at stone barns onto a farm track. Continue over the dismantled railway line, and after 30 paces bear right over a stream into open fields.

Now go immediately left, with the stream on your left and along the side of the hedge, heading generally southeast and through a hedge gap and across a gallop. In about 500yds (457m) the path arcs right away from the stream across a cultivated field to go over a footbridge. Carry on ahead up the left side of Stokeyleys Coppice (Point ❹).

At the corner of the coppice, go right along the waymarked footpath, beside the coppice. Beyond the coppice, the path bears slightly right to a mid-hedge footbridge by a waymark post, then crosses the middle of a large field to another waymark post. Continue ahead beside a hedge to go between houses in the village of Ettington. Go right along the main street of the village and, shortly after passing the former village hall and Village Store and Post Office, go left up Church Lane.

At the top of the lane you will be in Halford Road, with the Church of Holy Trinity and St Thomas of Canterbury to your right. Go left, then bear right into Rookery Lane. In about 300yds (274m), where the lane bends sharp left, proceed ahead over a stile. Pass to the right of Rookery Farm farm buildings on a metalled track, and turn right down the concrete farm track until you find the underpass for the A429. Go through the underpass and descend to a kissing gate.

Cross the field corner to another stile, then cross the next field diagonally. Go over the corner stile and continue ahead in a southwesterly direction over two cultivated fields to a country lane near Sotshole Coppice (Point ❸), reaching it via a stile and plank footbridge.

Go right along the lane for almost 200yds (183m), then turn right again over a stile and walk to the left of the field hedge. The clear footpath leads along the left-hand edge of Ettington Grove. At the end of the grove, bear right to cross a final cultivated field, then half right, until you come out near Grove Farm and rejoin Walk 28 at Point ❹. Go left along the farm track that proceeds to the left of woodland and complete the walk.

Meriden – the Traditional Centre of England

DISTANCE 5 miles (8km) MINIMUM TIME 2hrs 15min	
ASCENT/GRADIENT 197ft (60m) ▲▲▲ LEVEL OF DIFFICULTY ✦✦✦	
PATHS Field and woodland paths	
LANDSCAPE Gentle rolling countryside	
SUGGESTED MAP OS Explorer 221 Coventry & Warwick	
START/FINISH Grid reference: SP 251820	
DOG FRIENDLINESS Off lead through woodland, otherwise under strict control	
PARKING Old Road, Meriden, near The Queen's Head	
PUBLIC TOILETS None on route	

This easy walk offers the opportunity to visit an historic place and walk through some of the most attractive woodland in the area. Meriden is a pleasant commuter village providing quick access to Coventry and Birmingham along the busy A45. It is rumoured that Lady Godiva, wife of Earl Leofric of Mercia and owner of the village until AD 1066, founded the parish church of St Lawrence. You can see several timber-framed buildings and some moated farmsteads in the village, and it may be the site of an Iron Age field system.

Meriden claims to be the centre of England, and there is a sandstone pillar-shaped cross on the village green to mark the actual spot.

A TRIUMPH RECALLED

Meriden became home to Triumph motorcycles from 1941, after the factory in Coventry was destroyed by fire during World War II. In 1973 workers blockaded the factory to prevent closure, and subsequently formed a co-operative to buy it and market their motorcycles. In turn, Triumph Motorcycles (Meriden) Ltd eventually closed in 1983, and the factory was demolished the following year. The site has since been built over by a housing estate, with road names featuring Triumph motorbike model names. A plaque commemorating the Triumph Motorcycle Factory Meriden stands by Bonneville Close.

AN UNUSUAL WAR MEMORIAL

The National Cyclists' Memorial, dedicated to all those cyclists who gave their lives in both World Wars, can also be found on Meriden's village green. The memorial was erected with subscriptions from cyclists and cycling clubs and unveiled in May 1921 in the presence of over 20,000 cyclists. It was placed in Meriden to make it easy for cyclists to reach it from anywhere in the country, and is the site of an annual rally and commemorative service every May.

WOODMEN OF ARDEN

At 18th-century Forest Hall, to the west of Meriden, there is a piece of ancient turf where the Woodmen of Arden, the oldest archery society in England, holds its meetings. The turf is believed to have been undisturbed since the trees of the Forest of Arden first cast their shade over the archery butts. The society was established in 1785, and its membership is strictly limited to just 82 archers. There is also a horn here, said to have belonged to Robin Hood.

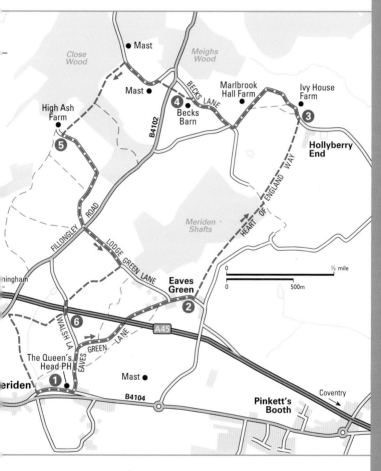

1 From The Queen's Head walk up Eaves Green Lane, following the Heart of England Way. Ignore Walsh Lane and continue right on Eaves Green Lane. Go beneath the A45 Birmingham–Coventry road and continue into the hamlet of Eaves Green. Continue ahead at the junction, on Showell Lane.

2 Pass a mobile home park and bear left through a kissing gate to a path that leads over meadows into Meriden Shafts woodland, via a footbridge and a kissing gate. Continue through another kissing gate and leave at its northeastern end via a further kissing gate. Go left along the track for 50 paces, then turn right into pastureland via a kissing gate. Continue ahead by the hedge-side, across three fields via a gate and a stile, and on to Harvest Hill Lane in Hollyberry End via another stile.

3 Go left on the lane past Ivy House Farm. The Heart of England Way leaves the route at a sharp left bend, but you stay on the lane. After passing Marlbrook Hall Farm, bear right at the next road junction to follow Becks Lane.

4 At Becks Barn go right of the drive via a stile to a waymarked path. Two gates lead through to a further kissing gate. Cross the road and the next field to a lane via a gate near two communication masts. Go along the lane, then left over a stile to a footpath to the left of Close Wood. Skirt a pond, and cross two stiles to enter the woodland. Leave Close Wood via another stile, and continue along the path over cultivated land.

5 Pass left of High Ash Farm and left of a Dutch barn, and descend to a kissing gate by a field gate. Through this bear right, descending a lane past Lodge Green House to the Fillongley road. Cross the road and continue down Lodge Green Lane opposite. Turn right over a stile, and take the path following a line of oak trees across a cultivated field. At the end, go over a stile to the road and turn left along Walsh Lane to a bridge over the A45.

6 Immediately across the bridge go right through a gate and take the path high above the A45. Go left through a gate into pastureland, heading for a footbridge to the right of a pond. Continue to the next field and a stile at the corner. Ignore the road and bear sharp left through a kissing gate to descend over several fields towards Meriden. Round the footpath crossing the drain at a footbridge and aim for the kissing gate. Go through this onto Old Road, and turn left to return to The Queen's Head.

WHERE TO EAT AND DRINK The Queen's Head is the favourite drinking hole for local walkers. It is on the Heart of England Way and offers a wide range of food, including a Thai menu. Children accompanied by adults are very welcome, but only guide dogs are allowed in the pub.

● ● ● ●

WHAT TO SEE Cross the B4202 and climb the hill to visit the Church of St Lawrence. From the churchyard you will be rewarded with fine views. If you stand near the ancient sundial or by the yew tree with the massive trunk you can see the city of Birmingham, and the view stretches out to the hills of Worcestershire, Staffordshire and Shropshire.

● ● ● ●

WHILE YOU'RE THERE The medieval cross in Meriden may not actually be the centre of England, as has been thought for over 500 years. Satellites and global positioning technology has recently identified that it is most likely to be in the middle of a farm field some 10 miles (16.1km) away but, to many people, Meriden will always remain the true centre.

Polesworth and the Coventry Canal

DISTANCE 5 miles (8km)	MINIMUM TIME 2hrs

ASCENT/GRADIENT 115ft (35m) ▲▲▲   LEVEL OF DIFFICULTY +++

PATHS Canal tow paths, field paths and residential areas

LANDSCAPE Gentle rolling farmland

SUGGESTED MAP OS Explorer 232 Nuneaton & Tamworth

START/FINISH Grid reference: SK 262024

DOG FRIENDLINESS Off lead along tow path, otherwise under control

PARKING Hall Court car park

PUBLIC TOILETS Near Fire Station, Tamworth Road, Polesworth

This trip to Polesworth allows you to experience a fragment of monastic England and to see a beautiful, ancient abbey church and vicarage (formerly the manor house). These buildings date back to AD 827 and form part of a nunnery built by Egbert, who is often claimed to have been the first Saxon king of all England. His daughter Editha was the abbess.

The abbey's dovecote can be found tucked away behind the village library. The superb 14th-century nunnery gate now has two residential flats in its upper storey. The larger of the two is said to be haunted by a friendly ghost. Apparently this harmless apparition moves plant pots around the building.

SQUIRES AND PAGES

The influence of the local squirearchy can be seen all around Polesworth. Nearby Pooley Hall was built by Sir Thomas Cockain in 1506, although there are records of an earlier Saxon hall on the site. The stones in the walls and the beams in the roof were taken from the ancient abbey, following its dissolution. Sir Henry Goodere became lord of the manor and there are stories connecting him with Michael Drayton (1563-1631), the poet, who was born in Hartshill. In his early years Drayton was a page-boy to Sir Henry at Pooley Hall, and William Shakespeare is said to have been a page-boy here too. Drayton was a regular companion of Shakespeare.

LARGE VILLAGE

Although the population of Polesworth has expanded to more than 9,000 people today, it retains a village atmosphere with its old part largely untouched and its many public houses intact. The River Anker and the Coventry Canal offer a quick step into the countryside, although it has been many years since local people were able to skate along these gentle backwaters. This used to be a favourite wintertime activity for villagers.

FIELDS AND TOW PATH

The walk starts near the library and takes you over the River Anker onto the tow path of the Coventry Canal. After the canal's bridge No. 49 you'll cross fields and lanes to the village of Dordon, before returning along Common Lane back into Polesworth.

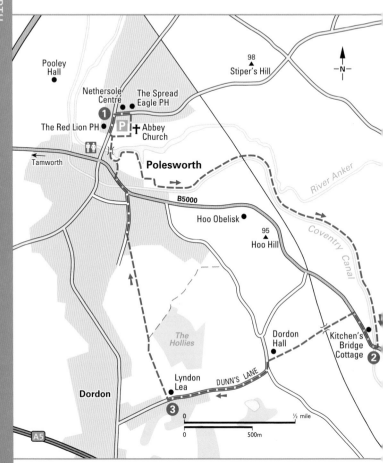

❶ From the car park at Hall Court, walk towards The Red Lion and left into Bridge Street, walking towards the bridge. After about 95 paces, turn left by the Spar shop into an alleyway that leads to a public footpath junction and turn right to take the path signed to the River Anker. Cross the footbridge over the river, then another, and bear left through the pleasant gardens, keeping by the river bank on a footpath. Leave the river and head for a sports pavilion. Beyond it turn left on a path beside

the bowling green that arcs gently right towards bridge No. 51 over the Coventry Canal. Descend to the canal and turn left along its pleasant tow path, which you now follow for the next 1.5 miles (2.4km). You may see fishermen trying to catch some of the perch, roach and chub in the canal. Before walking beneath the railway line look up to your right and on the far bank you will see the obelisk on Hoo Hill. Stiper's Hill is visible to the left. Continue beneath the main railway line and follow the tow path.

2 Leave the Coventry Canal's tow path when you get to bridge No. 49 and ascend onto the road, going left over the canal bridge and generally northwest past Kitchen's Bridge Cottage. Soon after passing the cottage, look out for a signposted hedge gap on the left and proceed through this to cross the footbridge over the railway line via two stiles. Now climb the hill, passing through the farm gate to the left of the buildings of Dordon Hall farm, and continue up to the road. Over a stile go left along the road, then soon turn right when you reach a road junction, following the signpost to Dordon. This will take you along Dunn's Lane into the village.

3 Immediately after passing a house called Lyndon Lea, at the crest of the hill, turn to the right down a track that leads to a gate onto a footpath over open farmland. Follow this footpath, heading generally northwards, towards the prominent trees of The Hollies. Continue left past the trees, crossing a stile. Ignore a kissing gate and continue ahead along a hedged path. Soon you will find yourself walking along a surfaced farm track that becomes Common Lane, on the approach to Polesworth village. Take the pavement of the lane through a residential estate until you reach the B5000 Tamworth–Grendon road. Turn left and cross the road with care, as it can be busy, and stroll over the canal bridge. Turn right at Polesworth Garage down to the park area by the River Anker and cross back over the footbridge. The public footpath now leads up to a junction of paths where you go right, towards the abbey. Bear left and leave through the Old Nunnery Gateway onto the High Street. Now turn left and continue along the High Street, past the Nethersole Centre and turn left again into Bridge Street to return to Hall Court car park.

WHERE TO EAT AND DRINK There are several good pubs in Polesworth and you will pass by a number along the route of the walk. The Spread Eagle and The Red Lion do not provide food, but the Fosters Yard pub on the corner of Market Street and Grendon Road will look after you well. The bar snacks and Pedigree real ale will appeal (children and dogs welcome).

● ● ● ●

WHAT TO SEE Look up to the right, midway through Point 1, for a close-up view of Hoo Obelisk on the far bank of the canal. This was originally erected in around 1848, close to the London Railway Line on the opposite side of the canal, but was moved in the 20th century for safety reasons. The inscription reads: 'Site of the Chapel of St Leonard at Hoo demolished 1538 30th Henry VIII'.

● ● ● ●

WHILE YOU'RE THERE Spare a little time to visit the old Abbey Church (closed Mondays) and see the 13th-century stone low-relief figure that is believed to be the effigy of the first abbess, Osanna. She lies on the tomb of Sir Richard Harthill with her feet on a stag, attired in a wimple and long straight gown with hanging sleeves. The church tower was built in memory of Harthill.

Around Charlecote and Wellesbourne

DISTANCE 6 miles (9.7km)	MINIMUM TIME 2hrs 15min
ASCENT/GRADIENT 33ft (10m) ▲ ▲ ▲	LEVEL OF DIFFICULTY ✦ ✦ ✦
PATHS Field paths and farm tracks	
LANDSCAPE Gentle rolling countryside	
SUGGESTED MAP OS Explorer 205 Stratford-upon-Avon	
START/FINISH Grid reference: SP 263564	
DOG FRIENDLINESS Under control at all times	
PARKING National Trust visitors car park for Charlecote Park (closed at night)	
PUBLIC TOILETS None on route	

This walk starts in the delightful village of Charlecote, about 5 miles (8km) from Stratford-upon-Avon. There is an opportunity to visit the superb Charlecote Park house (now managed by the National Trust), which has been the home of the Lucy family since 1247. The route passes along the banks of the pretty River Dene to the edge of the village of Wellesbourne and then crosses farmland and farm lanes on its return to Charlecote, passing close to 19th-century Charlecote Mill.

ELIZABETHAN JEWEL

Charlecote Park is an Elizabethan mansion that is largely hidden from the road by a fine parapeted gatehouse with an oriel window above its arch. The hall was rebuilt in 1558 by Sir Thomas Lucy, in the shape of the letter E, and is surrounded by a wonderful deer park. For more than 200 years fallow deer have been bred from stock and have roamed freely in the large park. Until recently some 250 fallow deer and 150 red deer (introduced by Henry Spencer Lucy in the 1840s) shared the park. Sadly, during 2001-02, an outbreak of bovine tuberculosis forced the estate managers to cull the entire herd. Thirty beasts were reintroduced in November 2002 and, while numbers have increased, the 100 or so Jacob sheep currently seem to have much of the huge park to themselves.

BARD NICKED

It was at Charlecote Park that a youthful William Shakespeare is alleged to have been arrested for deer poaching (often cited as the reason for his move from Stratford for London in the mid-1580s). The legend continues that the Bard got his own back on Sir Thomas Lucy and made him the butt of the world's laughter by depicting him as Mr Justice Shallow in *The Merry Wives of Windsor*. Doubters point to the fact the deer park had not yet been developed at Charlecote in Shakespeare's day. However, Thomas

Right: A view of Charlecote Park from the front gate (Walk 32)

Lucy was locally unpopular as a Justice of the Peace, and the subject of several mocking ballads being sung in the pubs of Stratford at the time. Shakespeare would certainly have known of these and could easily have adopted the caricature for his play.

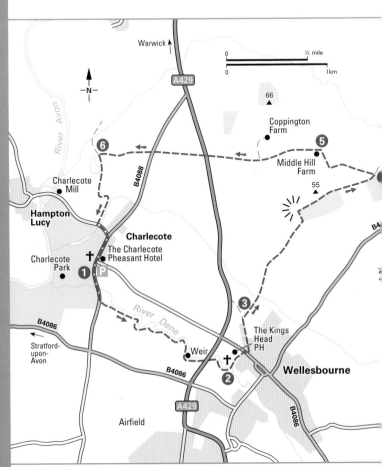

❶ From Charlecote Park car park, go left along the grass verge and cross over the River Dene. In about 100yds (91m), go left along a wide track that arcs left onto a clear fenced path by the side of the river. Follow this for about 1.5 miles (2.4km), passing a sewage farm, via a kissing gate, towards the village of Wellesbourne. You will pass a pleasant weir and go beneath the A429 before you come to a footbridge near St Peter's Church.

❷ Go left over the footbridge and up a fenced path into the churchyard.

Keep to the right of the church until you reach the village through the churchyard gates. Continue up the road to the left of house No. 21 – The Kings Head pub is on the left – then cross the main road in the village and walk up Warwick Road opposite.

❸ In about 300yds (274m), just after passing Daniell Road, go right along a tarmac path alongside modern houses. Cross a footbridge and, going through a kissing gate, continue ahead over a cultivated field. Through another kissing gate, continue ahead to cross a plank footbridge. Continue ahead along the left side of a hedge. Bear left across the field to go through a hedge gap and continue uphill to the left of the copse of trees. At the top of the rise, turn right and then go right into the woodland. Turn left along the clear track through the trees. You will emerge from the trees for a short distance and then re-enter. As the trees to the right thin out, look for a hedge gap to the left.

4 Go through the gap and cross a cultivated field to a hedge corner. Continue ahead alongside the hedge to a field corner, then bear right to Middle Hill Farm.

5 At a waymark post go left, between the farm buildings, then go to the right of the farmhouse and walk along the farm access lane for about 0.75 miles (1.2km), passing the entrance to Coppington Farm on the way to the A429. Cross the road with care and go over the stile

opposite onto a fenced footpath. After crossing another minor road, continue ahead along a concrete driveway to farm buildings.

6 Bear left between the buildings and then bear right through the gateway to follow the field boundary on the right. Turn left at a kissing gate (don't go through it) to a second kissing gate which leads into a large cultivated field that you walk around by the field hedge, initially alongside a long lake. Go right, through a further kissing gate, and continue to the right of the field hedge until you go through a final kissing gate onto Charlecote Road. Go left along the footway past a delightful thatched cottage into the centre of Charlecote, then turn right along the grass verge of the main street, passing the half-timbered houses and The Charlecote Pheasant Hotel, with St Leonard's Church opposite, to reach the Charlecote Park car park.

WHERE TO EAT AND DRINK The Charlecote Pheasant Hotel has a fine lounge, can cater easily for large numbers and offers an excellent carvery. In Wellesbourne the walking route goes close to The Kings Head pub. Children are allowed, but dogs are restricted to the gardens.

• • • •

WHAT TO SEE As well as visiting Charlecote Park, take some time to explore the village of Wellesbourne. Seek out Chestnut Square in Wellesbourne Mountford and the thatched pub, The Stags Head, in a corner. A plaque in the bus shelter records that it was here, in 1872, that Joseph Arch inaugurated the first trade union for agricultural workers. The event is remembered with an annual parade.

• • • •

WHILE YOU'RE THERE Visit Charlecote Mill and observe the 19th-century mill grind corn by waterpower. There has been a mill on the site since the Norman Conquest, but the present one was built in about 1800. It stopped grinding corn by waterpower in 1939 but in 1983 it was acquired by the present owner, who restored it and brought it back into full time use. Open 11am–5pm, first Sunday of every month from April to October.

Exploring Warwick

DISTANCE 5 miles (8km)	MINIMUM TIME 2hrs

ASCENT/GRADIENT 33ft (10m) ▲▲▲   LEVEL OF DIFFICULTY ✦✦✦

PATHS Canal and riverside paths, street pavements

LANDSCAPE Canalside and historic town

SUGGESTED MAP OS Explorer 221 Coventry & Warwick

START/FINISH Grid reference: SP 277647

DOG FRIENDLINESS Off lead along tow path, otherwise under control

PARKING Racecourse car park (St Mary's Area 3 car park, at north end of racecourse, pay-and-display)

PUBLIC TOILETS None on route

This easy walk offers the opportunity to visit one of the most famous castles in England. Starting from the car park at Warwick Racecourse, a stroll along the tow path of the Grand Union Canal to the River Avon brings you to Castle Bridge. This offers the classic view of Warwick Castle.

FORTRESS HOME

Built in the 14th century, Warwick Castle sits imperiously above the River Avon near the centre of the town. It is the ancestral home of the Earls of Warwick, of whom Richard Beauchamp (1428–71) was probably the most famous. He lived through the reigns of three kings and was present at the burning of Joan of Arc.

You can spend a whole day at Warwick Castle, there is so much to see: the Bailey, Guy's Tower (128ft/39m high), Caesar's Tower (147ft/45m high), the Gatehouse, the Clock Tower and the Old Bridge over the River Avon are all truly superb. Inside you can see the tapestry of the gardens of Versailles, Cromwell's helmet and Queen Anne's travelling trunk. Outside, there are gardens that were designed by Lancelot 'Capability' Brown in the 18th century.

Tear yourself away from the castle to continue the walk, through the county town of 'Shakespeare Country'. It displays a fascinating blend of Georgian and Tudor architecture. In Castle Street you pass the timbered home of Thomas Oken – now housing a doll museum (see What to See). St Mary's Church is up the road opposite. You can climb its great 174ft (53m) tower for a fantastic view over the town and the surrounding countryside. Inside the church is the 15th-century Beauchamp Chapel where the body of Richard Beauchamp lies. Near by in St Mary's is the tomb of Ambrose Dudley, Earl of Leicester – it is said to have been made by the same craftsmen who modelled Shakespeare's bust at Stratford.

Before heading back to the racecourse you'll pass Lord Leycester's Hospital. This was originally the Guild House of St George, which became the Almshouse in 1571, founded by Robert Dudley.

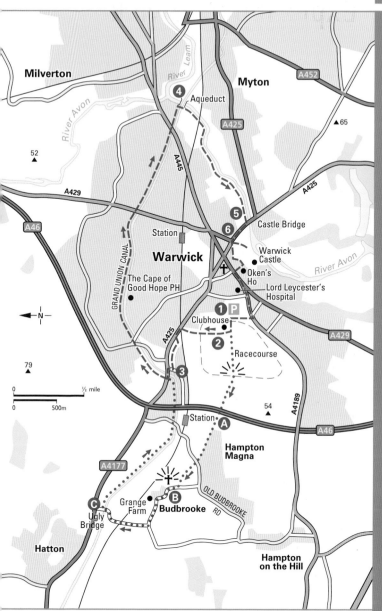

1 Walk to the end of the racecourse car park and go left towards the golf clubhouse, the Warwick Golf Centre.

2 Beyond, go right and take the wide green track between the golf course and the driving range. In about 300yds (274m), cross over the

racetrack and go through a kissing gate onto a footpath alongside modern housing. Continue ahead, and at the corner of common land go right through a kissing gate onto a lane, and descend to the road. Go left along the pavement beneath the railway bridge, then left opposite

St Michael's Road through a gate (locked 6pm–8am) onto grassland by the Saltisford Canal. Follow this grassy area to the tow path, passing a large narrowboat mooring area, and climb the steps up to the canal bridge onto the pavement beside a road. Go right along the pavement, and in 50yds (46m) you will come to a canal bridge over the Grand Union Canal and the busy A425.

3 Cross the road with care. Go left over the canal bridge and, immediately across it, descend to take the tow path into Warwick, about 1.5 miles (2.4km) away. Pass a lock gate with The Cape of Good Hope pub opposite, and along the back of residential properties. Shortly after passing by a Tesco store and just before reaching the aqueduct over the River Avon, go left down steps to join the 'Waterside Walk', turning right at the stream.

4 Proceed right under the aqueduct and follow the riverbank footpath. At Castle Bridge, climb steps onto the pavement of the A425 (Banbury) road and cross with care.

5 Stroll onto the bridge for the classic view of Warwick Castle, then turn around and follow the pavement towards Warwick town.

6 In 220yds (201m) go left and meander down picturesque Mill Street for the second favourite view of the castle. Return to the main road and go left through the main entrance gate to Warwick Castle grounds. Walk up the drive to the main gate, turn right up steps, pass the castle entrance and turn left on Castle Lane. Turn right on Castle Street and continue, passing Oken's House, to reach the tourist information centre on the corner of the High Street. Turn left here and walk along High Street, going beneath the archway of the Lord Leycester Hospital. Go right into Bowling Green Street, and in 50yds (46m) turn left down Friars Street to return to the St Mary's Area 3 car park.

WHERE TO EAT AND DRINK Along the route The Cape of Good Hope by the side of the Grand Union Canal is a popular pub with walkers – children and dogs are welcomed. It has a patio overlooking the canal and serves bar snacks and good ale.

● ● ● ●

WHAT TO SEE As you walk up Castle Street you pass a pretty, timber-framed 15th-century house. This is Thomas Oken's House. Oken was a silk and luxury goods merchant and a famous Warwick benefactor. He founded an almshouse for poor women, endowed a schoolmaster and provided money for bonfires for the young. He was Master of the Guild at the time of the 1545 town charter.

● ● ● ●

WHILE YOUR'E THERE No trip to Warwick is complete without a visit to Warwick Castle, but do walk carefully as you enter the eerie Ghost Tower for you may not be alone. It was here, in 1628, that Sir Fulke Greville was fatally stabbed by a manservant, angry that he did not bequeath sufficient funds to him in his will.

Right: The view to Warwick Castle from the River Avon (Walk 33)

A Loop from Warwick to Budbrooke

DISTANCE 8 miles (12.9km)   **MINIMUM TIME** 3 hrs

ASCENT/GRADIENT 69ft (21m) ▲▲▲   **LEVEL OF DIFFICULTY** +++

SEE MAP AND INFORMATION PANEL FOR WALK 33

From the golf driving range building (near Point **2**), continue ahead on the clearly waymarked footpath, walking in a northwesterly direction. Before crossing the racetrack pause to enjoy a fine view back over Warwick. Cross over the footbridge, go through a handgate on the right and continue across pastureland, alongside a hedge, to a stile. When you reach the hedge by the busy A46, go over a stile and through a kissing gate to cross the road with care. Go through another kissing gate, and follow the footpath to the left of the field hedge, climbing towards the village of Hampton Magna (Point **A**). Over a stile, the footpath takes you past a residential estate onto the Old Budbrooke Road via another stile. Look out for the large stone recalling the history of the Warwickshire Regiment, whose barracks were once located here at the small village of Budbrooke.

Cross the road and a footbridge, go through a kissing gate and continue on through a kissing gate leading into meadowland. The footpath arcs right, passing a pond, then veers left over a footbridge, and through another kissing gate towards the church in Budbrooke (Point **B**). Through a kissing gate and gate, you reach the 13th-century parish church which contains a marble monument to Rowland Dormer. Grove Park, the home of the Dormers, an influential family, is located in wooded parkland near by. From the church there is a grand view of Warwick town, with the tower of St Mary's and the castle prominent amid the trees. There are also several memorials to the fallen soldiers of the Warwickshire Regiment.

Go right through the churchyard and through a gate onto a lane. Go right again along the lane past Grange Farm and under the railway line to reach Ugly Bridge over the Grand Union Canal (Point **C**). Pause on the bridge and look northwest up the canal to see the attractive row of Hatton Lockgates. There are 21 lock gates and the canal rises some 140ft (42m) over 2 miles (3.2km). You may be lucky enough to see a narrowboat making its way down the flight of locks. Now descend to the tow path and follow it, going southeast towards Warwick.

After passing by six lock gates, including Hatton Bottom Lock (near Warwick Parkway railway station), rejoin the main walk by the A425 at Point **3**.

At Kenilworth Castle

DISTANCE 4.5 miles (7.2km)	MINIMUM TIME 2hrs 15min
ASCENT/GRADIENT 105ft (32m) ▲▲▲	LEVEL OF DIFFICULTY +++
PATHS Field paths and farm tracks	
LANDSCAPE Rolling countryside	
SUGGESTED MAP OS Explorer 221 Coventry & Warwick	
START/FINISH Grid reference: SP 279723	
DOG FRIENDLINESS On lead at all times	
PARKING In front of castle by Castle Green	
PUBLIC TOILETS None on route	
NOTES Walk extended to 5.5miles (8.8km) if you visit Honiley Church	

The dramatic ruins of Kenilworth Castle are an important part of English history. This walk starts from the castle and goes over farmland, then circles around Chase Wood to return along a track from where the best views of the castle ruins can be enjoyed. Extend the walk a little by visiting Honiley Church, rebuilt in 1707 to a design sketched – if legend can be believed – by the great architect, Christopher Wren.

FROM FORTRESS TO CASTLE

Kenilworth Castle was the stronghold for lords and kings of England in the 11th and 12th centuries. Originally it was a timber fortress, and King John paid several visits to the castle, spending £1,115 between 1210 and 1216 rebuilding the outer bailey wall in stone and improving the other defences. In the 14th century John of Gaunt transformed it into a grand castle, building a great hall.

The castle later passed to Henry IV. Henry V rested here after his victory at Agincourt in 1415, and it remained a royal residence until Queen Elizabeth I gave it to her favourite courtier, Robert Dudley, in 1563. It was then used to host a series of lavish entertainments for the Queen. The Civil War brought about its demise when, after a long siege, Cromwell ordered the defences to be dismantled. The romantic ruin became a tourist destination from the 18th century onwards, and its popular fame was sealed when it became the setting for large parts of the action in Sir Walter Scott's historical novel *Kenilworth* (1826).

A PLEASANCE PLACE

Pleasance Mound, 'The Pleasance in the Marsh,' lies northwest of the castle. A moated, timber-framed manor house was built here for Henry V in around 1414, at the edge of the Great Mere – an artificial lake which formed part of the castle defences. The site was primarily used as pleasure garden and place of entertainment in preference to the castle's more formal state apartments.

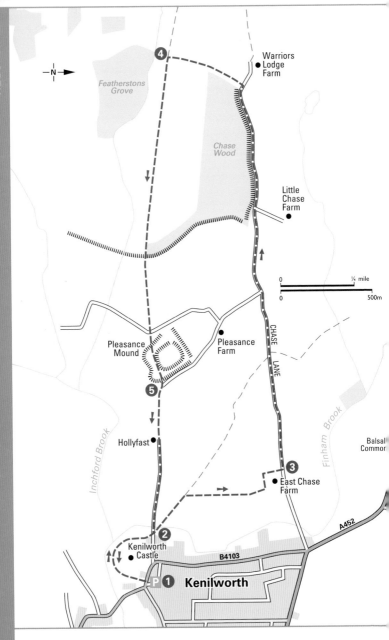

❶ Walk towards the castle from the car park and go through the kissing gate to the left of the impressive ruins. Take the footpath that circles around the foot of the castle walls, climbing up to and crossing over the causeway, then descending to go

through a kissing gate. Go ahead to pass to the left of a beautiful cream-painted thatched cottage, and then onto a good wide track. Go left along this track for 120yds (110m), then turn right through a kissing gate into a cultivated field.

2 Follow the well-walked footpath diagonally across the field. When you reach the field corner turn round to enjoy the fine view of the castle behind, then leave the main footpath by going right and heading up a less-used green track, heading north. Walk ahead along this track over several fields and through a kissing gate. Pass to the left of East Chase Farm. Continue past the barns and hen run enclosure and then veer right towards a stile.

3 Cross the stile and head left along Chase Lane for the next 1.5 miles (2.4km) before passing to the right of Chase Wood. At the wood end, turn left on a stony farm track. After about 400yds (366m) reach a junction of footpaths. To your right you will see Honiley Church (the footpath leading there and back will add about a further mile (1.6km) to your route).

4 At the junction of footpaths, go left along a fine, wide grass track to the right of the field hedge, with Chase Wood further to the left. Follow this straight track for about 0.5 miles (800m), going over a footbridge. Go through two kissing gates, and continue over the Pleasance Mound earthworks to go through a further kissing gate. As you leave, you will pass an information board about the excavation.

5 Walk along the hedged footpath that leads to the farm drive to Hollyfast. Continue ahead along the drive. As you reach the brow of the hill you can enjoy another classic view of Kenilworth Castle. This spectacular view continues as you descend the other side of the hill. Just before reaching the thatched cottage again, turn right onto a well-walked footpath that circles around the walls of the castle. Pass through a kissing gate and cross the castle causeway, then descend the footpath leading back to the car park.

WHERE TO EAT AND DRINK There is a tear room for visitors to the castle. Otherwise, The Queen and Castle, and The Clarendon Arms by Castle Green in Kenilworth are two popular eating places.

● ● ● ●

WHAT TO SEE If you complete this walk in the spring you can expect to see a carpet of bluebells in Chase Wood. Look out for the views of Kenilworth Castle as you complete the walk and pause from time to time at different points along the walk. After draining part of the lake around the castle, Henry V built a summer house on 'The Pleasance' – can you spot the site?

● ● ● ●

WHILE YOU'RE THERE Explore the Elizabethan garden at Kenilworth Castle. Based on contemporary drawings, this is a recreation (2009) by English Heritage of the original terrace gardens designed for Robert Dudley, complete with formal paths between geometric beds, and four dramatic, spiky obelisks. There's also an elegant aviary, and a central fountain.

Long Compton and the Rollright Stones

DISTANCE 5 miles (8km)	MINIMUM TIME 2hrs

ASCENT/GRADIENT 673ft (205m) ▲▲▲   LEVEL OF DIFFICULTY ✦✦✦

PATHS Field paths and country lanes

LANDSCAPE Rolling countryside on edge of Cotswold Hills

SUGGESTED MAP OS Explorer 191 Banbury, Bicester & Chipping Norton

START/FINISH Grid reference: SP 289323

DOG FRIENDLINESS Under control at all times

PARKING Near Red Lion, Long Compton (ask permission from the hotel)

PUBLIC TOILETS None on route

This short, hilly walk offers the chance to visit the Rollright Stones, set up on the hills on the county border with Oxfordshire. The walk starts from Long Compton and ascends the lane up towards Little Rollright. The route passes by the famous stones and returns over farmland into the picturesque village of Little Rollright before descending back into Long Compton. This is a pleasant village through which the A3400 winds its way between Stratford-upon-Avon and Oxford. You may be enchanted by the fine old stone houses that line the road and the unusual lychgate to the village church. This was once a 16th-century cottage from which the lower storey has been removed. It appears like a two-storey gatehouse with an arch beneath. The old church has loopholes which may have been used by marksmen during the Civil War.

BRONZE AGE STONE CIRCLE

The Rollright Stones comprise some 60 monoliths positioned in three sets. The King Stone is on the Warwickshire side of the road while the Whispering Knights and the group called the King's Men are on the other side, in Oxfordshire. The stones, which are much older than those found at Stonehenge, are all worn rough by the winds and centuries of rain. The King Stone is the largest at nearly 9ft (2.75m), and this is said to be placed in such a position that when seen from the centre of the King's Men circle on 21 June, the rising sun is immediately in line with the stone. The stones in the King's Men circle measure from between 4ft (1.2m) to 7ft (2.1m).

WITCH MEETS KING

Long Compton is well known for its witches, and it is not surprising that the ancient stones are surrounded by legend. The most well known of these suggests that the stones were once human – a king, his knights and their followers. The king is said to have encountered a witch close to where the stones stand. She told him to take seven strides to the top of the hill, pronouncing, 'If Long Compton thou canst see, King of England shalt thou be!" When the eager king got to the top of the hill, he couldn't see Long Compton because a spur of land obstructed the view. The witch then turned the monarch and his hapless followers all to stone – thus creating the King Stone and the King's Men. The Whispering Knights are said to have been traitors who were plotting against the King.

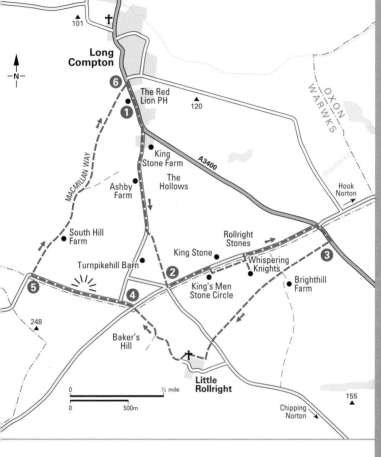

❶ From The Red Lion go right, along the A3400 through Long Compton. Where the road bends sharp left, turn right and walk up Little Rollright Road, passing King Stone Farm and Ashby Farm as you climb an area known as The Hollows. After about 0.5 miles (800m) the road bends slightly to the right, and here you go left and immediately onto a footpath with Turnpikehill Barn away to your right. Ascend the footpath to the lane near to the Rollright Stones.

❷ Go left along the lane to the famous stones. In just over 0.25 miles (400m), go right through a kissing gate and you will find the King's Men stone circle on the right, with King Stone in the field on the left. After looking at the King's Men stone circle, continue along a grassy permissive path parallel to the road for a further 500yds (457m), then bear right along the footpath to see the third group of stones, called the Whispering Knights. Return to the road and turn right to continue along it for about another 0.5 miles (800m), then at the A3400 junction go to the right and at the brow of the hill go right again up nine steps to a field.

3 Continue ahead along a grassy path, the hedge on your left, over two fields to a stile. Cross the driveway to Brighthill Farm, and continue ahead through a copse to a double stile. Continue ahead across a cultivated field, then follow a field edge track that descends to a lane. Cross this and descend to Little Rollright via two kissing gates. At a lane turn right to curve north to the superb church. From the church ascend the footpath, signed 'Little Compton Footpath Only', up Baker's Hill to the road.

4 Over a stile cross the road to follow the lane opposite for the next 0.5 miles (800m) towards Little Compton, enjoying the view to the right over Long Compton and towards the village of Brailes.

5 Where the road bends left, go right over a stone stile (not straight onto the bridleway track) and continue ahead over a cultivated field in a generally northeast direction – the view ahead is superb. Descend to the left of South Hill Farm, and continue walking on the MacMillan Way path over several fields, passing through two gates and over a stile. The path becomes a surfaced road. Just after passing to the right of farm buildings, go left and over a stile, then continue ahead via another stile down into Long Compton. Leave the footpath through two pairs of farm gates to arrive back in the village.

6 Go right along the road and return to The Red Lion car park.

WHERE TO EAT AND DRINK The Red Lion Hotel at the start is the only pub on this route. It's a popular eating place with walkers and visitors to the area, offering parking, good food, comfortable accommodation, excellent ales and fine gardens.

● ● ● ●

WHAT TO SEE Five miles (8km) southwest of Long Compton is Chastleton House, probably England's finest Jacobean house. The building has soaring gables and an elaborate state bedroom containing 'Queen Elizabeth's bed'. In the Cavaliers' Room, find out the story of Captain Arthur Jones who, on his return from the Battle of Worcester in 1651, was mistaken by Roundheads for Charles II. Admission to this National Trust property is by timed ticket.

● ● ● ●

WHILE YOU'RE THERE At nearby Hook Norton, 6 miles (9.7km) to the east, you will find the Hook Norton Brewery. In this part of England, Hook Norton ales are king, and the buildings at the brewery are a treat to see and visit. Here you can find out about hummellers, chondrometers, saccharometers and wort coolers. Call (01608) 730384 to arrange a tour of this famous local brewery.

Lower Brailes and Sutton-under-Brailes

DISTANCE 5 miles (8km)	MINIMUM TIME 1hr 30min

ASCENT/GRADIENT 476ft (145m) ▲▲▲   LEVEL OF DIFFICULTY +++

PATHS Field paths and country lanes

LANDSCAPE Rolling hills

SUGGESTED MAP OS Explorer 191 Banbury, Bicester & Chipping Norton

START/FINISH Grid reference: SP 308394

DOG FRIENDLINESS Under control at all times

PARKING Village Hall car park in Lower Brailes – donation to hall funds expected

PUBLIC TOILETS None on route

In medieval times Brailes was the third-largest town in Warwickshire. Today it comprises a pair of small country villages, happily situated off main routes, away from the hustle and bustle of the modern towns and cities. This fine walk takes you over part of Brailes Hill which, at 761ft (232m), is the second-highest point in Warwickshire. From the pretty village of Upper Brailes you walk into Lower Brailes and can enjoy lovely views as you descend into open countryside. You climb above Sutton Brook and will have a wonderful valley view as you go down to Sutton-under-Brailes.

EXPLORING THE BRAILES

It is a delight to walk through the old part of Upper Brailes, where there are a number of thatched cottages, and an ancient earthwork and burial ground called Castle Hill. Following the arrival of the Normans in the 11th century, it was used as the basis for a conventional castle of the motte-and-bailey style. Now it is an excellent vantage point for those who wish to play 'King of the Castle'. From the top of its hill you can see the distinctive marks of the medieval ridge-and-furrow cultivation methods in the surrounding fields.

Lower Brailes is also a dreamy place and, although it has no castle, it does contain the 14th-century Church of St George. With its splendid 120ft (37m) tower, it is sometimes a referred to as the 'Cathedral of the Feldon', a potentially baffling claim to fame until you learn that 'Feldon' is an old English word for an area of rich, fertile farmland. It is without a doubt one of the finest churches in Warwickshire. Inside you'll find some exquisite illuminated manuscripts. These date from the middle of the 13th century and are the work of William de Brailes and Matthew Paris.

Brailes has attracted its fair share of unusual and interesting characters. Nance Austin gained a reputation as the Brailes witch. Apparently she specialised in levitation and had a familiar in the form of a cat. Richard Davies was a worthy Elizabethan scholar who is remembered in a monument above a tomb of black marble in St George's Church.

Field paths lead you around the slopes of Brailes Hill between these three lovely villages, which reward you for taking time to explore on foot.

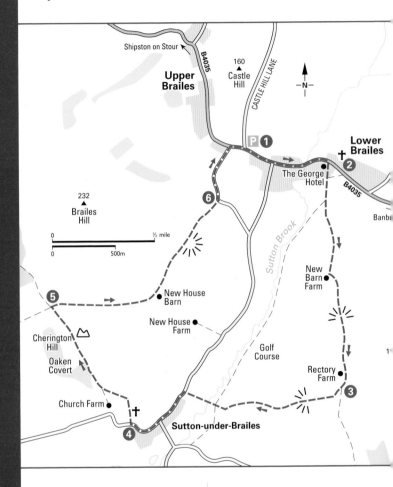

1 Leave the car park by the village hall in Lower Brailes to join the B4035. Turn left to stroll up through the beautiful village for about 0.5 miles (800m), passing The George Hotel, which has always been popular with local ramblers (see Where to Eat and Drink) and now houses the village post office.

2 Turn right and walk down a waymarked public footpath just beyond The George Hotel. This runs

beside a small Cotswold dry-stone wall, passing over a low stile, and then through a gate to cross Cow Lane into pastureland via a stile. Continue ahead, and at a footpath junction waymark post continue ahead to a double stile and footbridge in the hedge. Cross them and bear half right to the next stile, then quarter left for two further fields via a stile by a footbridge between them, heading for New Barn Farm. The footpath goes to the left of the farm complex to a handgate. Through this, continue alongside the hedge to another gate. Beyond continue half left up the hill, crossing the field to a footbridge and stile. Cross the corner of the next field and continue ahead on the right-hand side of the hedge – there is a good view back over Lower Brailes. Walk up the path, then go through a hedge gap and bear right, walking above the trees surrounding the ruinous Rectory Farm.

3 Bear right at the end of the trees then half left, and now begin a gentle descent on a farm track, enjoying a wonderful view ahead over the valley as you proceed towards Sutton-under-Brailes. Pass through a field gate, the golf course now to your right, and when you reach the road at the bottom of the hill, turn left and wander through this beautiful Cotswold village, going to the right, past the village green, and heading for a stile to the left-hand side of the parish church and Church Cottage.

4 Clamber over the stile, then another, to cross an orchard and walk past the church. Go through a kissing gate and head half left across the cultivated field by Church Farm. Go through a kissing gate in the far corner onto a farm lane. Turn right up this track, passing to the right-hand side of Oaken Covert. Continue ahead through a field gate and uphill alongside a post-and-wire fence. Pass through another field gate, and with a hedge on your right you ascend Cherington Hill.

5 Just past three pine trees you reach a junction of public footpaths. Go right through a metal bridle gate and follow a tractor track heading generally eastwards. The route goes to the left-hand side of New House Barn. Continue ahead through a field gate along a track, through another gate, and continue along the top of a farm field, with more good views over the Brailes Valley to the right. At end of the field go through a handgate to descend the hedged track called High Lane, the lower part a deep sunken lane, to reach Tommy's Turn.

6 Turn left and walk down the lane, continuing your descent into Henbrook Lane. Soon you will come back out onto the High Street in Lower Brailes (the B4035). Turn right along the road for about 100yds (91m) to return to the village hall car park on the corner of Castle Hill Lane.

WHERE TO EAT AND DRINK The George Hotel, in the middle of Lower Brailes, has long been a popular eating and drinking place for local walkers and walking groups. Apart from fine local ales and excellent home-made food, there is a large rear garden to enjoy.

WHAT TO SEE In the quaint village of Sutton-under-Brailes, time appears to have stood still. Attractive houses surround the picturesque village green and the fine old tombs in the churchyard lie beneath a magnificent spreading chestnut tree. The 13th-century church has a beautiful, lofty tower and a 14th- to 15th-century porch. There is a shallow recess on its north side which may once have been a chantry chapel.

At Hartshill Hayes

DISTANCE 4.5 miles (7.2km)   MINIMUM TIME 1hr 45min

ASCENT/GRADIENT 295ft (90m) ▲▲▲   LEVEL OF DIFFICULTY ✦✦✦

PATHS Lanes, field paths, woodland tracks and tow paths

LANDSCAPE Country park and rolling countryside

SUGGESTED MAP OS Explorer 232 Nuneaton & Tamworth

START/FINISH Grid reference: SP 317943

DOG FRIENDLINESS Off lead in park and along tow path

PARKING Hartshill Hayes Country Park, pay-and-display

PUBLIC TOILETS Hartshill Hayes Country Park

In 1978, around 136 acres (55ha) of the hillside around Hartshill were made into the fine country park which forms the basis of this walk. It strays into Warwickshire proper and includes part of the Coventry Canal. A sizeable area of woodland has developed at Hartshill, refreshingly dominated by traditional broadleaved trees such as oak, beech, sycamore, hazel and alder. Elder and holly also thrive.

Hartshill village is an old settlement, but there is little information to establish its full history. The Romans were here and may have built a military station on the hill. Hugh de Hardreshull built a motte-and-bailey castle on the hill in 1125. Robert de Hartshill, who became Lord of the Castle, was killed alongside Simon de Montfort at the battle of Evesham in 1265. Perhaps it fell into disuse then, for all traces of the fortification have long since disappeared.

The village's most famous resident was the poet Michael Drayton, a contemporary and friend of William Shakespeare. He was born in 1563 at the long demolished Chapel Cottage in Hartshill Green, and there is a plaque in his memory. His poem *A Fine Day* suggests he drew considerable inspiration from the local landscape:

'Clear had the day been from the dawn
All chequered was the sky
Thin clouds like scarfs of cobweb lawn
Veiled heaven's most glorious eye.'

In *Polyolbion* he described the River Anker, which weaves its way past his birthplace to join the River Tame, as 'trifling betwixt her banks so slow'.

THRIVING CANALSIDE SCENE

The Coventry Canal came long after Drayton's day. It winds along the valley linking Atherstone and the Fazeley Junction, where it joins the main canal system to connect with the Trent and Mersey.

The canal reached Fazeley in 1790, happily coinciding with the completion date of the Oxford Canal and allowing it to improve a shaky financial position (its construction had run massively over budget). It remained in a reasonably sound state until 1948, when nationalisation was followed by disuse and deterioration. In recent years, however, it has been successfully restored for pleasure craft.

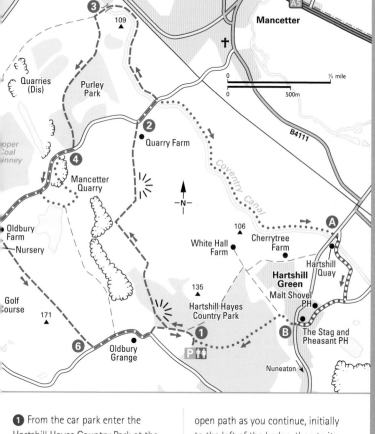

1 From the car park enter the Hartshill Hayes Country Park at the back of the visitor centre. Pass the children's play area and take the path which arcs left (northwest) along the top of Hartshill, alongside a covered reservoir, and enjoy the super view over the surrounding area. Continue ahead across the greensward on the path that then descends right into woodland. At the bottom of the woodland go over the two footbridges and then bear left to walk along a fine

open path as you continue, initially to the left of the hedge, then to its right. In about 0.25 miles (400m) the path bends to the right and you will ascend northeast to the brow of the hill, from where you can overlook the Coventry Canal and get a great view. Bear left beside a kissing gate onto the path, which becomes hedged as you progress northwards towards Quarry Farm. Go through the gate to the left of the farm buildings onto Quarry Lane.

② Turn right and stroll down the lane, bearing right at the junction until you come to bridge No. 36 over the Coventry Canal. Cross either bridge and descend right to the tow path. Go right under the bridge to walk in a northwesterly direction, and in 0.5 miles (800m) proceed beneath bridge No. 37.

③ Leave the tow path at bridge No. 38 and cross the canal onto a quiet lane. Walk up the lane for about 150yds (137m) then, just before a private house, go left through a tall kissing gate into meadowland and on into pastureland. Cross over the footbridge at the bottom of the field, then walk half right across the next field and on to a gate. This leads to a footbridge and a second tall kissing gate, and you enter the woodland of Purley Park. Follow the footpath up the right edge of the woodland. The path arcs left into the trees and you will exit on to Quarry Lane again.

④ Go right and head up the lane, past the entrance to Mancetter Quarry (see While You're There). Continue along the lane and in a further 600yds (549m), just past Oldbury Farm, go left.

⑤ Walk to the right of the farm buildings, with market gardens on your right, to reach a good bridlepath beside ponds going southeast. This lovely path crosses arable land, but soon you will be following yellow-topped marker posts across a golf course.

⑥ Exit onto a road, via a gate, and then go left. The road passes by Oldbury Grange and Oldbury Grange Gardens. Where there is a sharp right-hand bend in the road, go left up towards the rear entrance to the gardens and enter Hartshill Hayes Country Park via two gates. Once you are in the park bear right and join the waymarked park path that takes you back to the visitor centre.

WHERE TO EAT AND DRINK At peak times there is a snack bar at the country park car park. In nearby Hartshill Green you'll find The Malt Shovel and The Stag and Pheasant pubs. Both serve food and are welcoming to walkers. Children and dogs may be allowed in certain rooms only.

• • • •

WHAT TO SEE As you return to the country park the walk takes you past Oldbury Grange, now a nursing home, which was built around 1904 by Garside Phillips, the first manager of Ansley Colliery. He bought it for his son Joseph, who himself became 'The Boss' at the pit. The Phillips family became the leading gentry in the village. Joseph's grandson is Captain Mark Phillips, the renowned horseman and former husband of Princess Anne.

• • • •

WHILE YOU'RE THERE Follow the permissive footpath near Point 4 into Mancetter Quarry. There are art installations, new planting and interpretive panels explaining the development and future of these dramatic quarry workings. You can return to the main route by following the footpath to the right from a junction. In Hartshill Green, a blue plaque on a block of flats marks the site of the Shakespearean poet Michael Drayton's birthplace.

Hartshill Hayes and the Coventry Canal

DISTANCE 4.5 miles (7.2km)   MINIMUM TIME 2hrs

ASCENT/GRADIENT 262ft (80m) ▲▲▲   LEVEL OF DIFFICULTY +++

SEE MAP AND INFORMATION PANEL FOR WALK 38

Once over canal bridge No. 36 and on the tow path, just after Point ②, go left (southeast) along the Coventry Canal. As you stroll along there are fine views to the east and up towards Hartshill Hayes Country Park (see Walk 38). Walk along the tow path until you come to bridge No. 32, where the old Hartshill Quay maintenance yard has retained its clock tower.

Pass under the bridge (Point Ⓐ) and bear left up the bank, turning right over a second bridge (No. 32). Follow the quiet lane past the old toll cottage then walk on, as it bears right, up the hill away from the canal. At a junction turn right, continuing on this road into Hartshill Green. Look for the interpretive panel on the right which explains the importance of quarry working in this area. Continue past The Malt Shovel pub and turn right at the junction, walking past The Stag and Pheasant pub to reach the main road. Cross over and locate a footpath to the right of Drayton Court flats (Point Ⓑ).

Go down the steep steps, crossing a long footbridge and then entering the woodland of Hartshill Hayes. Walk up the waymarked path through the deciduous trees, always staying on the main route. The path arcs generally towards the northwest. Bear right at a stone seat. Eventually turn left to emerge from the trees, via a kissing gate, onto the main path in the park. Bear left and return to the car park at Point ①.

A Coventry City Tour

DISTANCE 3 miles (4.8km)   MINIMUM TIME 1hr 30min

ASCENT/GRADIENT 16ft (5m) ▲▲▲   LEVEL OF DIFFICULTY ✦✦✦

PATHS Street pavements

LANDSCAPE Historic Coventry

SUGGESTED MAP AA Street by Street: West Midlands

START/FINISH Grid reference: SP 335789

DOG FRIENDLINESS On lead at all times

PARKING Any park-and-ride car park, then travel into city centre by bus

PUBLIC TOILETS Library Building in Smithford Way

This short but inspiring tour guides you around the most historic parts of Coventry's centre, starting at Old St Michael's Cathedral. This became a cathedral in 1918, as a replacement for St Mary's, which had been abandoned after the Reformation. It was severely damaged in the bombing raid of 14 November 1940, when so much of the city was destroyed, and it's shell remains as a memorial to that dark time.

Basil Spence was the the clear winner of the 1950 competition to design a new cathedral, and his stark modern design has been the subject of much controversy over the years. It was a radical new approach and a complete break away from traditional style. The new cathedral was finally consecrated in May 1962 in the presence of Queen Elizabeth II, and you can compare ancient with modern during your walk.

ST MARY'S GUILDHALL

Another impressive and important building which is well worth exploring is St Mary's Guildhall on Bayley Lane. After fleeing from London during the Wars of the Roses in 1456, King Henry VI and Queen Margaret spent most of their time in Coventry, where St Mary's Guildhall became the prime venue for entertaining royalty and their court. Amongst its many functions, the guildhall has also been extensively used as a theatre. Its raised dais made the hall suitable for public performance, and over the years it became a regular venue for visiting players. William Shakespeare is known to have performed here as a young actor in 1580. Shakespeare's last visit to Coventry was in 1608, and as you walk past the guildhall you can see a statue of the Bard above the main archway.

CALLING A HUSBAND'S BLUFF

Lady Godiva is one of the more remarkable names associated with Coventry. Godiva was the wife of Leofric, Earl of Mercia, one of the most powerful Anglo-Saxon noblemen in 11th-century England. Leofric became so exasperated by Godiva's endless appeals to reduce Coventry's heavy and punitive taxes that he declared he would do so if she rode naked through the crowded marketplace. Boldly, Godiva did exactly that – with her flowing hair covering all of her body except her legs. You will see a statue of her on her horse as you pass through the main shopping precinct.

A MEDIEVAL MASTERPIECE

Along the walk is Cheylesmore Manor House, which dates from the 13th century and has been lovingly renovated over the centuries by the City of Coventry. It is an outstanding example of a house from this period. It once belonged to Queen Isabella (the wife of Edward II) and in 1338 was passed to her grandson, Edward, the Black Prince.

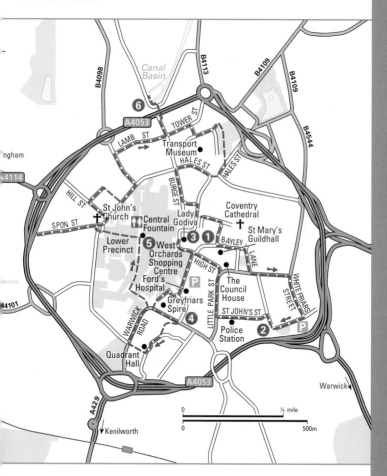

❶ From the tourist information office, go left down Bayley Lane, past St Mary's Guildhall. Turn right into Earl Street, then left into Jordan Well. Cross the road and go right, down Whitefriars Street. At the bottom, just before the car park, go right along cobbled Whitefriars Lane, to pass beneath Whitefriars Gateway.

Overleaf: Ruins of Coventry's Old St Michael's Cathedral (Walk 40)

2 Turn right into Much Park Street, then take the first left turn, along St John's Street to Little Park Street. Turn right down here, then left in front of the mock-Tudor Council House. Continue left along the High Street, past the Cathedral Lanes Shopping Centre, to the Lady Godiva statue.

3 Walk back towards the High Street and go right down Greyfriars Lane. After the car park is the row of restored almshouses, Ford's Hospital. Continue along Greyfriars Lane and take the pathway to the right of the 230-ft (70m) Greyfriars Spire – all that remains of the 14th-century Church of Christ Church – to New Union Street. Go left and cross at the crossing through the Manor Yard archway, to Cheylesmore Manor.

4 At Manor House Drive go right, and just past Quadrant Hall, go right again down a footpath to Warwick Road. Cross Warwick Road and turn right to the shopping precinct at Bull Yard. Go left into Shelton Square, then bear right and continue along Market Way into the centre of the main shopping area.

5 By the fountain, go left into Lower Precinct. At the traffic island by St John's Church, cross the road and walk down Spon Street, to admire the row of medieval buildings. At the end retrace your steps past St John's Church, and turn left into Hill Street. On your left is the Old Bablake School, founded in 1560 for the education of poor boys of Coventry. Go right along Bond Street and through the archway by Olan Mills, left into Corporation Street. Turn left into Upper Well Street, then right into Lamb Street. Turn left to a footbridge over The Ringway that leads to the Canal Basin.

6 Retrace your steps over the footbridge and walk down Bishop Street. Turn left along Tower Street, right down to Cook Street, and left alongside the rear of the Transport Museum. After going beneath 15th-century Cook Street Gateway, turn right and stroll through Lady Herbert's Garden to Hales Street by the Swanswell (Priory) Gate. Pass in front of the Transport Museum right along Hales Street to a junction. Turn left up The Burges, then left around Ironmonger Row and cross the road. Go right and then left into Priory Row and down between the New and the Old Cathedrals to return to the tourist information office.

WHERE TO EAT AND DRINK The route of this walk takes you past several of Coventry's best pubs, including The Old Windmill and The Shakespeare in Spon Street, The Town Wall Tavern in Bond Street, The Tudor Rose in The Burges and the Golden Cross in Hay Lane.

WHAT TO SEE Coventry is a city undergoing a lot of redevelopment but the old historic parts are being preserved. Obtain a free street guide/map from the tourist information office before you begin your walk. There is also a very helpful booklet explaining the detailed history of each building you will pass by or visit.

Edgehill and Ratley

DISTANCE 6 miles (9.7km)	MINIMUM TIME 2hrs 30min

ASCENT/GRADIENT 164ft (50m) ▲▲▲　　LEVEL OF DIFFICULTY +++

PATHS Lanes and field paths

LANDSCAPE Rolling countryside

SUGGESTED MAP OS Explorer 206 Edge Hill & Fenny Compton

START/FINISH Grid reference: SP 362458

DOG FRIENDLINESS On lead at all times

PARKING At lay-by on A422

PUBLIC TOILETS None on route

This hilly walk takes you along the escarpment of the famous Edgehill – a prominent sandstone ridge which runs from northeast to southwest at a height of around 600ft (183m) above sea level.

FIRST OF MANY BATTLES

Below the ridge, on the land which stretches away towards Kineton, the first major battle of the Civil War took place in October 1642. It pitted the cavaliers of King Charles I against a poorly equipped Parliamentarian army under Robert Devereux, Earl of Essex. Prince Rupert led the charge of the King's cavalry on his galloping white charger, as he would throughout the coming campaign, but on this day the outcome was inconclusive. The fighting petered out when darkness fell, the Royalists hastening back towards Banbury, the Parliamentarians to Warwick. Neither side could claim a victory. Entering the field with some 14,000 men apiece, they departed leaving around 3,000 casualties in total, and lost perhaps as many men again as deserters. You can't visit the actual battle site today, as it is hidden in a huge Ministry of Defence ammunition facility, but an Edgehill Battle Museum can be found in the grounds of Farnborough House, some 3 miles (4.8km) to the east.

The splendid Radway Tower, passed towards the end of the walk, was constructed to mark the 100th anniversary of the battle, though it wasn't completed until 1750. This 70ft (21m) octagonal folly is now occupied by the popular Castle Inn.

VIEWS FROM THE RIDGE

There are other monuments and views to be seen from the ridge. From Ratley you can see an obelisk erected in 1854 by Charles Chambers to commemorate the Battle of Waterloo. At Nadbury Camp the mounds of an 18-acre (7ha) Bronze Age camp can still be seen, although the remains have been dissected by a busy road and there has been considerable damage by ploughing. The walk also takes you close to the National Trust's Upton House before descending into the medieval village of Ratley.

You'll find Ratley is a peaceful village, set away from the main Oxford road and largely unchanged since the turn of the 20th century. Its recognition in 1971 as a conservation area has helped ensure the survival of its oldest parts. Records show the manor was held by a Saxon named Ordic, before the arrival of the Normans. Most of its houses are built of honey-brown Hornton stone – a local limestone produced in the Edgehill quarry. Quarrying was once a major local industry. Today the quarried land has been reclaimed, planted with trees and has become a nature reserve.

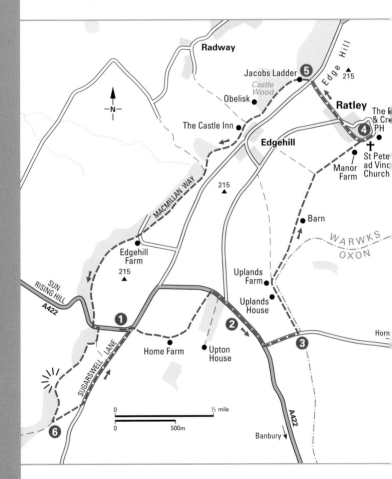

❶ From the lay-by on the A422 walk east, go left and in 10yds (9m) go right again through a farm gate, following a stone wall. Then, through another gate, bear left towards Home Farm. Pass to the left of the farm buildings, then go left and aim for the far right corner of the field and two kissing gates. Continue ahead via a kissing gate through the National Trust car park to another gate and the A422. Go right along the grass verge of the busy road past the entrance gates to the 17th-century Upton House.

❷ In about 600yds (549m), cross the A422 with care and go left down the lane to Hornton.

3 In a further 300yds (274m), nearly opposite Quarry Cottage, go left along a signed path. Walk to the left of the field hedge over two fields, then pass to the right of the buildings of Uplands House and Uplands Farm. Continue over a stile into open countryside, bearing right beyond a wire fence down a track to a farm gate and stile, and descend into the valley. Walk by the hedge and pass to the left of an old, dilapidated barn. Cross a stile and ascend to a junction of paths. Go left through a gate and immediately over a stile to continue ahead, descending a farm field to reach another stile in the far right corner. Head steeply half left and descend to a stone stile, to emerge in Ratley village by Manor Farm.

4 At the main road turn right to explore the old village, then retrace your steps past Manor Farm and continue straight ahead along the road towards Edge Hill.

5 Cross over the road at the T-junction and descend the many steps of Jacobs Ladder into Castle Wood opposite, following the waymarkers of the MacMillan Way, and ignoring the gate into open countryside. Take the footpath along the escarpment of the famous hill. After about 0.25 miles (400m) of walking take a right fork and shortly look right to see the Obelisk. Continue along the escarpment path, passing below The Castle Inn. Stay on this path, waymarked Macmillan Way and Centenary Way for about 1.25 miles (2km), sometimes in the edge of the wood and sometimes with the hedge on your left and trees on your right. Keep on the MacMillan Way until you reach the A422, at the top of Sun Rising Hill. Turn left along the road for about 50 paces and go right along the concrete track, initially bearing right at stables, then left before taking the footpath on the right into a copse. Soon pass through a gate to open land with a superb view of Tysoe and the surrounding countryside. Continue through a second gate and follow a path on the edge of the woods for about 300yds (274m).

6 Go left through a farm gate and diagonally left across the field to reach Sugarswell Lane via a handgate. Continue left along the lane to the A422 and the lay-by.

WHERE TO EAT AND DRINK The Castle Inn in Edgehill is a splendid castellated public house. The mock castle was built as a gatehouse between 1742 and 1750 to commemorate the centenary of the Battle of Edgehill. Its design is based on Guy's Tower at Warwick Castle, with a wooden drawbridge linking its 70-ft (21m) tower with a smaller one.

● ● ● ●

WHAT TO SEE While in Ratley take a look at the Church of St Peter ad Vincula – 'St Peter in Chains' (this refers to his imprisonment recorded in the Acts of the Apostles, Chapter 12). One of its brass memorial plates tells us that the heiress of Simon Bury died on the 14th February, Anno Domini 1696 aged 1697. Even in the 17th century typographical mistakes were made!

Where Canals Meet at Hawkesbury Junction

DISTANCE 4.5 miles (7.2km)	**MINIMUM TIME** 1hr 45min

ASCENT/GRADIENT 56ft (17m) ▲▲▲   **LEVEL OF DIFFICULTY** +++

PATHS Lanes, field paths, woodland tracks and tow paths

LANDSCAPE Canalside and gentle countryside

SUGGESTED MAP OS Explorer 221 Coventry & Warwick

START/FINISH Grid reference: SP 361844

DOG FRIENDLINESS Off lead along tow path, otherwise under control

PARKING Near Greyhound pub at Hawkesbury Junction

PUBLIC TOILETS None on route

This easy walk gives you the opportunity to share a Midlands canal experience by walking the tow paths of two of the area's most important canals. They formed an important link in Britain's network of canals during the Industrial Revolution.

The route takes you from Hawkesbury Junction to Hawkesbury village, and then through pleasant countryside to reach the Coventry Way. After passing newly constructed Hollyhurst fishery and Coalpit Fields Woodlands Nature Reserve, you join the Coventry Canal near Bedworth. Although it is quiet now, this was once a major coalmining community. You start and finish in the Hawkesbury Junction conservation area, where the elegant 50-ft (15m) Britannia Foundry of Derby's cast-iron bridge, built in 1837, spans the junction of the Coventry and Oxford canals.

THE COVENTRY AND OXFORD CANALS

Hawkesbury Junction was also known as Sutton Stop, after the name of the first lock keeper. It became a famous resting place for bargees on this part of the canal system. In 1821 an engine house was built to pump water up into the canal from a local well. The Newcomen-type atmospheric steam engine which lifted the well water was called Lady Godiva. It ceased pumping in 1913 and has since been transferred to the Newcomen Engine House museum in Dartmouth, Devon. Thomas Newcomen was born in Dartmouth in 1663, and Lady Godiva forms the centrepiece of his memorial museum. At Hawkesbury Junction, The Greyhound Inn and the pump house are reminders of this once busy scene. Photographers will find a classic shot through the archway of the cast-iron bridge.

GRAND TRUNK OBJECTIVE

The Act of Parliament to enable construction of the Coventry Canal was passed in 1768 with two objectives. The first aim was to connect Coventry with a new trade route called the Grand Trunk (today known as the Trent and Mersey Canal). The second was to provide Coventry with cheap coal from the coalfield at Bedworth, a major mining community. By 1769 the stretch of canal between Coventry and Bedworth had been completed, but because of some wrangling with the Oxford Canal Company the Coventry Canal did not reach its point of linkage with the Grand Trunk at Fazeley until 1790. James Brindley was the original engineer for this attractive contour canal, but he was sacked from the job following an overspend of authorised capital.

COALS TO LONDON

Brindley was also the engineer of the winding 91-mile (146km) Oxford Canal, one of the earliest to be built. Its objective was to connect the Midlands with London. It reached Oxford in 1789 and was completed in 1790. Initially the link was achieved with the Coventry Canal via a mile-long (1.6km) parallel stretch of canal. In 1801 the Hawkesbury Junction was constructed to avoid this costly duplication. The price of coal in the capital, which was previously transported from Newcastle by sea, dropped almost immediately.

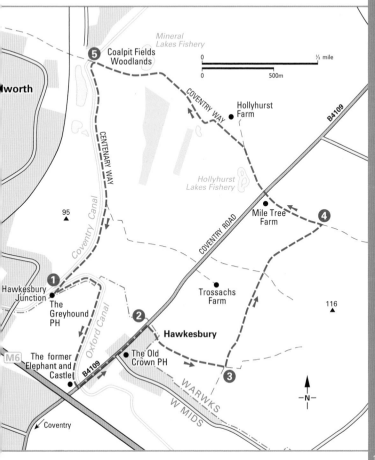

1 After parking in Sutton Stop, walk past The Greyhound pub and continue along the Oxford Canal tow path. Walk beneath the electricity pylons and leave the canal at the first road bridge beside a house, formerly The Elephant and Castle pub. Go left, crossing the bridge over the Oxford Canal, and follow Coventry Road past The Old Crown.

2 In about 250yds (229m), just before the large sign for Bedworth and Nuneaton, go right and take the footpath into meadowland. Continue along the footpath to a stile, then go left over the stile into a large field. Cross the field, heading towards a double stile at the end, but don't go over the stile.

3 Go left again and head towards another stile in the field corner. Cross this and continue in a northeasterly direction over two stiles and through three field gates. Your route passes by Trossachs Farm (on the left) and you continue along the path by the field edge. After going over a stile and footbridge, walk diagonally over a large field, aiming to the left of an ash tree in the far corner.

4 Go over the stile, then bear sharp left to join the Coventry Way. Take the track by the field edge until you exit onto the Coventry road once again via a stile, near to Mile Tree Farm. Cross the road to a sign for Hollyhurst Lakes and continue ahead on a track, heading past fishing lakes generally towards Hollyhurst Farm. Follow the Coventry Way as the path arcs left at a waymark post, and follow a hedged path. Soon, through a pair of kissing gates, bear left onto a grassy track which curves right alongside Coalpit Fields Woodlands. Go left over a stile and bear right along a farm track to reach bridge No. 13 over the Coventry Canal.

5 Just before reaching the bridge, go left and descend to the tow path along the pleasant canal for about a mile (1.6km). Head south along the tow path – this is part of the Centenary Way. The path arcs gently right (southwest), and soon you reach Hawkesbury Junction where large numbers of colourful narrowboats are usually moored and The Greyhound pub offers a welcome break. Cross the cast-iron footbridge to reach the pub and the end of the walk.

WHERE TO EAT AND DRINK The walk passes The Old Crown in Hawkesbury village. The Greyhound at Hawkebury Junction is attractively placed and has large gardens where children and dogs are allowed. Tables outside offer views of the canal basin.

● ● ● ●

WHAT TO SEE The canals are heavily used by local anglers, usually with rods much taller than themselves. You may see pike, roach, perch, bream or carp being hauled onto the bank. If you stroll off the main route at Bedworth Hill Bridge you can visit two small lakes where, apparently, the fish are even bigger!

● ● ● ●

WHILE YOU'RE THERE Spend a little time at Hawkesbury Junction enjoying the magical scene with its traditionally decorated narrowboats, as their occupants visit the chandlery (or The Greyhound) or manoeuvre between the two canals.

Harbury, Chesterton and the Lakes

DISTANCE 4 miles (6.4km)		MINIMUM TIME 1hr 45min	

ASCENT/GRADIENT 131ft (40m) ▲▲▲   LEVEL OF DIFFICULTY ✦✦✦

PATHS Farm driveways and field paths

LANDSCAPE Rolling Warwickshire countryside

SUGGESTED MAP OS Explorer 206 Edge Hill & Fenny Compton

START/FINISH Grid reference: SP 373597

DOG FRIENDLINESS Under control at all times

PARKING Village hall car park in Harbury (closed overnight)

PUBLIC TOILETS None on route

This walk starts from one of the most historic places in Warwickshire, for Harbury was once the home of a huge ichthyosaurus that roamed the local countryside. Its skeleton and those of a plesiosaurus and several marine dinosaurs have been found in the old quarries here, as have Bronze Age cooking pots.

In about 500 BC there was an Iron Age camp (or byrig) in these parts. It was ruled by a woman called Hereburh, and Harbury's name derives from 'the fortified place belonging to a woman called Hereburh'. The Romans were also here. Their great Fosse Way forms one of the boundaries to the village, and Roman culverts can still be seen. Ridge and furrow fields reveal evidence of Saxon farmers, and an area called Temple End suggests the land was once owned by the Knights Templar.

MINOR POETS

The parish church of All Saints is mostly Norman and dates from the 13th century. It sports a sundial carrying the accusatory inscription 'Tyme flyeth, what doest thou?' The Wagstaffes were the 'proprietors' of the manor from the time of Henry VIII (1491–1547), and inside the church is a memorial to Jane Wagstaffe who lived here during Elizabeth I's reign. Behind the church is the Tudor 'Wagstaffe School' which was founded by Jane's descendants in 1611. The vicar from 1746 to 1771 was Richard Jago, a minor poet. Today, Harbury is a delightful old village to enjoy.

From Harbury, the walk takes you south along peaceful country lanes, passing by attractive lakes to reach the tiny hamlet of Chesterton – a place of rare beauty where time appears to have stood still. The name of the hamlet is of Roman origin. The village was hit very badly by the plague of 1349, and by the 15th century there were only three families residing here. It has recovered a little since then, but much of its former extent has survived for archaeologists to discover.

SPECIAL CHURCH

Today there is no shop or pub in this lovely hamlet, but St Giles' Church is rather special. Its battlemented parapet runs the entire length of the chancel, and is set on walls which are 3ft (0.9m) thick. It was founded by Richard the Forester and was presented to the priory at Kenilworth in Richard II's time (1377–99). Sir Edward Peyto built the wonderful landmark four-sail windmill. The return route takes you over pastureland and cultivated fields, passing by an old metal windpump before reaching Harbury village.

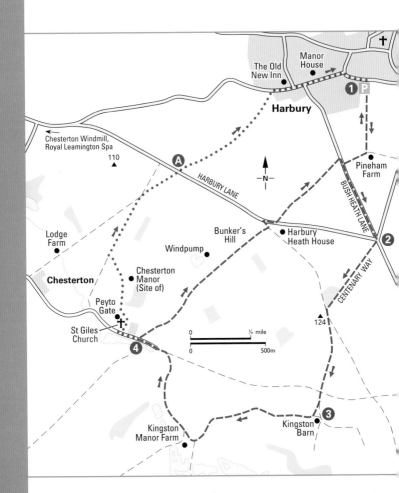

❶ Leave the car park behind the village hall and head south by football pitches to a gate in the far corner. Don't go through it, but bear right to follow the waymarkers for the Centenary Way. Cross a field to a second gate onto Bush Heath Lane. Turn left and walk down to a junction of lanes.

❷ Go right here, signed 'Kingston Farm', over a cattle grid and along the grass verge of a driveway for about 600yds (549m), still following the Centenary Way. Where the Way goes off to the left, continue ahead along a quiet country lane. Soon the buildings of Kingston Barn farm will be to your left, but fork right to follow the lane as it goes to the right of the farm complex, to reach a lane going off to the right by a footpath guide post.

❸ Proceed right along this lane, which weaves its way through some very attractive countryside with long views of Chesterton windmill. When you reach the garden walls to Kingston Manor Farm, turn right again and continue along the lane, now heading in a northwesterly direction, passing some lakes. After about 0.5 miles (800m) of easy walking past the picturesque lakes, the lane arcs left up towards St Giles' Church in the hamlet of Chesterton. Through a gate or over a cattle grid, continue up the lane towards the church.

❹ Some 120 paces before reaching the church gate, go right through a kissing gate and ascend over cultivated fields and pastureland, following the footpaths and heading generally northeast back towards Harbury. The footpath crosses a stile and passes to the right of an old wind pump and Bunker's Hill. Over the brow of the hill head towards the left-hand of a group of houses, then left along the field edge to a gate onto Harbury Lane, near Harbury Heath House. Turn right, and after 100yds (91m) turn left through a metal gate on a footpath that initially is to the right of the field hedge and later to the left, until you reach Bush Heath Lane. Go through a gate and turn right onto a lane, then after about 30 paces go left through a gate to rejoin the Centenary Way once again. The path leads towards Pineham Farm. After about 200yds (183m), go left beside a gate to return to the car park at the back of Harbury village hall.

WHERE TO EAT AND DRINK You are spoilt for choice for pubs in Harbury, where good food, fine ale and a cheerful reception are always available. Choose from The Crown Inn in Crown Street, The Gamecock on the corner of Chapel Street, The Dog Inn and The Old New Inn in Temple End, and The Shakespeare Inn, a 16th-century part-timber framed inn close to the sail-less 18th-century windmill in the middle of the village.

● ● ● ●

WHAT TO SEE Visit the 12th-century St Giles' Church in Chesterton. The sundial over its porch offers advice to travellers: 'See and be gone about your business.' The oldest part is now the 14th-century nave. The church is inextricably linked to the Peyto family who owned the Manor House on the hill at the back of the church. Their tombs are impressive. There is a 16th-century alabaster memorial to Humphrey Peyto and his wife Anna, with effigies of their ten children. Sir Edward Peyto supported Cromwell's Parliamentarians and successfully led the defence of Warwick Castle against the Royalists.

● ● ● ●

WHILE YOU'RE THERE Visit the unique Chesterton Windmill, by Harbury Lane on Windmill Hill. The windmill was probably designed by Sir Edward Peyto himself in 1632 (and influenced by Inigo Jones), and was built as a tower supported on six semicircular arches. It was used up until 1910 and contains the original machinery, which dates from 1860. It is usually open on only one weekend a year.

Harbury and Chesterton

DISTANCE 5 miles (8km)   MINIMUM TIME 2hrs 15min

ASCENT/GRADIENT 180ft (55m) ▲▲▲   LEVEL OF DIFFICULTY ✦✦✦

SEE MAP AND INFORMATION PANEL FOR WALK 43

This short extension to Walk 43 explores some of Chesterton. It is recommended that you get hold of a copy of the leaflet *Discover Chesterton – A Journey Through Time,* produced by the Warwickshire Archaeology Research Team. It provides a map showing the many historic locations around Chesterton.

When you reach Chesterton leave Walk 43 at Point ❹ and continue along the lane. Soon pass through the entrance gate to St Giles' Church (see What to See, Walk 43).

The path goes to the right of the church, and you leave the churchyard through the handgate in the far corner, to the right of a small shed, and well to the right of the ornamental Peyto gateway in the north churchyard wall. (This is a copy of one designed by Inigo Jones and built to provide a suitable entry for the Peyto family.)

Descend the field and, passing to the left of a reed-filled pond, go over the footbridge, with a stile at each end, in the hedge below, then over another stile into the next field. Head straight uphill, and at the brow aim to the left of some rather derelict buildings – the remains of outbuildings to Chesterton Manor, largely demolished in 1802.

In the valley to the left are the buildings of Lodge Farm. Southwest of these are the remains of a medieval settlement, identified as Netherend in a document of 1319.

Go through the handgate and then right, through a second. A third handgate leads into a large field which you cross going northeast towards a handgate in the fence ahead – the site of the manor house is to the right of here.

Through a gate, take the right of two paths, heading to the far right-hand corner of a large field, following the waymark direction. Via a handgate and footbridge, exit on to Harbury Lane (Point Ⓐ). Cross the lane, go over a footbridge and through a kissing gate and maintain your direction over several fields, passing through kissing gates, over footbridges and through gates until you emerge through another gate by a house in Temple End, in Harbury. Go right along the road and you will pass by The Old New Inn and the Manor House as you progress into Park Lane. Bear right into South Parade, to return to the car park at the rear of the village hall (Point ❶).

From certain positions on this walk Chesterton Windmill comes into view. There are no footpaths to provide a link route to the windmill, but access is possible from a permissive path off a nearby road.

Left: Chesterton Windmill at sunrise (Walks 43 and 44)

Eathorpe and Wappenbury

DISTANCE 3.5 miles (5.7km)	MINIMUM TIME 1hr 30min	

ASCENT/GRADIENT 82ft (25m) ▲▲▲   LEVEL OF DIFFICULTY ✦✦✦

PATHS Mainly field footpaths and farm tracks

LANDSCAPE Gentle countryside

SUGGESTED MAP OS Explorer 221 Coventry & Warwick

START/FINISH Grid reference: SP 392689

DOG FRIENDLINESS Under control at all times

PARKING Village hall car park in Eathorpe or along road near by

PUBLIC TOILETS None on route

This is a stroll through the attractive hidden villages southeast of Coventry. The route starts at Eathorpe, going near to the River Leam and over pleasant Warwickshire countryside to the historic village of Wappenbury, then crosses the river to Hunningham before returning to Eathorpe along an unclassified road.

EATHORPE AND ITS HALLS

The name is derived from 'ea' relating to water and 'thorpe', which is a common Old Norse suffix that usually denotes a farmstead. The village is sandwiched between the old Fosse Way – the Roman Road from Lincoln to Axminster in Devon – and the River Leam.

Eathorpe has two halls: the excellent Village Hall (with its small car park) which was built in 2006, and the grander mansion of Eathorpe Hall which is set in secluded parkland south of the village centre. This is a large 18th-century red-brick house once owned by Samuel Shepheard, who built the famous Shepheard's Hotel in Cairo. Less grandly, he also rebuilt the bridge across the River Leam, which bears a commemorative inscription noting its completion date of 1862.

WAPPENBURY

Early records show a variety of names for the village of Wappenbury but it is likely that it means 'Wappa's fortified place'. It was certainly once fortified, and the great earthwork ramparts can still be seen here, best preserved on the northwestern and eastern sides. Archaeologists date the great earthwork to the first century AD, some 900 years before the Danish leader Wappa came on the scene. The rampart remains surround the whole village and are believed to be the largest in the Midlands. It is assumed it was constructed to control fords across the River Leam. During excavations, four kilns dating to about AD 350 have been found, along with some items of Roman greyware. We have no reason to doubt that the village thrived into the Middle Ages, but then, like so many others in the area, the plague came, taking the lives of some 200 villagers. Wappenbury has never recovered its original size.

The Church of St John the Baptist has a 15th-century tower, and two coffin lids are the oldest stones in the village. Gravestones and murals make fascinating reading.

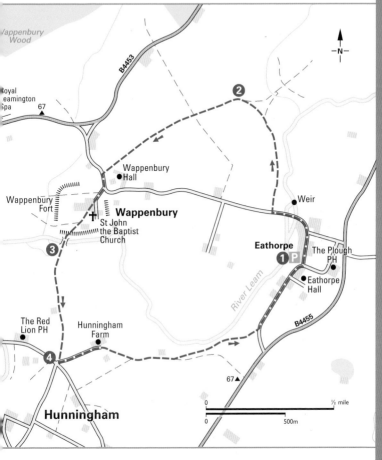

1 From the Village Hall head through the village, initially passing a lovely pair of 17th-century thatched dwellings called Myrtle and Thyme Cottages. At the end of the village the road bends left to pass the old watermill, and crosses the bridge over the River Leam. In around 80yds (73m), go right through a kissing gate into pastureland and follow the footpath to the left of the river. You will reach a fence with a distant view of Princethorpe College, with its fine turrets. Cross the stile and aim for the handgate in the

far left corner of the field beside a farm gate.

2 Through the gate, follow the waymarker direction, with the hedge on your right. Continue ahead via a kissing gate at a footpath junction and alongside a hedge, with wooded grounds on the crest ahead. Go through a field gate and continue ahead to a kissing gate to the right of some conifers. Continue alongside trees until you come to a handgate at the road into Wappenbury, to the right of the walls of Wappenbury

Hall's grounds. Turn left along the village road until you come to the front gates of Wappenbury Hall. Go right here towards the Church of St John the Baptist – to its left you will see thatched Garden Cottage. Walk along the lane to the right of the church and continue right, by a laurel hedge, passing to the right of converted farm buildings. Head back into the open countryside. Go left at a footpath fork through a gate onto a footpath. Descend to a gate onto a single-arch brick bridge, with a second (metal) footbridge beyond it.

❸ Across the River Leam there is about 0.5 miles (800m) of easy walking. Passing through two gates, you reach the road in the village of Hunningham via a bridle gate. To visit The Red Lion pub turn right through the village for 0.25 miles (400m). The pub garden looks towards the narrow, partly medieval bridge over the River Leam, mostly rebuilt around 1651.

❹ If you do not visit the pub, go left and walk up the farm drive towards Hunningham Farm, signed 'Leam Lodge and Unclassified County Road'. Continue between the farm buildings, the road now no more than a good stone farm track. After following this road for about 600yds (549m), you will see that it bends to the right about 80 paces ahead of you. Look out for a stile here, leading onto a footpath going off to the left towards the River Leam once again. Walk along the footpath close to the riverbank. From the river the footpath veers right through a kissing gate. Continue along the edge of the field and left at the corner over two stiles. Veer right, and leave the next field over a stile beside an oak tree. Here you are back to the road on the edge of Eathorpe. Go left along the road, passing the entrance to Eathorpe Hall and its lodge to return to the village.

WHERE TO EAT AND DRINK The Plough in Eathorpe is a regular haunt for walking groups. Good food and good ale are the order of the day. At The Red Lion in Hunningham, chicken with cranberry and other delicious home-made meals may appeal. Children are allowed in both pubs, but dogs are restricted to the large gardens.

● ● ● ●

WHAT TO SEE Explore the village of Wappenbury, with its idyllic thatched cottages. Impressive Wappenbury Hall was once the home of Sir William Lyons, the founder of Jaguar Motors. In the Church of St John the Baptist, see the canopied wall monument of a woman sitting sadly in a harvest field – this is a memorial to Thomas Urnbers, a patron of 19th-century scientific agriculture.

● ● ● ●

WHILE YOU'RE THERE Just four miles (6.4km) to the north of Eathorpe is the 100-acre (40ha) Ryton Pools Country Park. It's a good place to spot water birds – look especially for great crested grebes, swans, moorhens and Canada geese on Ryton Pool. Pagets Pool attracts dragonflies, and there are often as many as 17 species around the lake. Look out for the common blue and emperor dragonfly and the black-tailed skimmer.

Around the Dassetts

DISTANCE 7.25 miles (11.7km)	**MINIMUM TIME** 3hrs 15min
ASCENT/GRADIENT 656ft (200m) ▲▲▲	**LEVEL OF DIFFICULTY** +++

PATHS Field paths and farm tracks

LANDSCAPE Hilly countryside

SUGGESTED MAP OS Explorer 206 Edge Hill & Fenny Compton

START/FINISH Grid reference: SP 394523

DOG FRIENDLINESS Under control at all times; many stiles

PARKING Burton Dassett Hills Country Park car park

PUBLIC TOILETS Near car park

This lovely walk takes you from the very top of the Dassett Hills in the Burton Dassett Hills Country Park, and through the nearby hamlets and villages of Northend, Fenny Compton, Farnborough, Avon Dassett and Burton Dassett. It's the nearest you will get in Warwickshire to wild country, with its bare hills reminiscent of the Peak District. The 100-acre (40ha) country park was opened in 1971, and is set high above the noisy M40 motorway, which didn't arrive until a couple of decades later. The park comprises a dramatic mix of rugged, grassy humps and hills with a quaint, small beacon perched on the highest point – actually the tower of a former windmill. There are a number of quarries around the side of the hills which may date back as far as the Iron Age. Today they are covered in grass and offer welcome shelter for picnicking visitors. The view from the top of the hills is outstanding.

A WATERING HOLE OR TWO

Initially the walk descends into Northend hamlet, before field paths lead you into the village of Fenny Compton. Fenny is an unusual, but not infrequent, prefix in the Midlands and indicates the presence of wetland. The village lies below the Dassett Hills, which give rise to at least seven springs. It was to harness these, to supply around 40 consumers in the village, that one of England's smallest water supply companies was established in 1866.

You pass by several very attractive cottages to reach the impressive Church of St Peter and St Clare – only two churches in England carry this unusual dedication. The walk continues over Windmill Hill, offering fine views over the surrounding countryside. You then descend into the village of Farnborough and find more old stone cottages and The Inn (see Where to Eat and Drink). After the village of Avon Dassett, the walk then ascends into Burton Dassett, passing by the tiny 12th-century All Saints Church.

The hills of the Burton Dassett Hills Country Park have been a constant theme throughout this walk and you finish with a flourish on the last of them, Magpie Hill, to enjoy the extensive views.

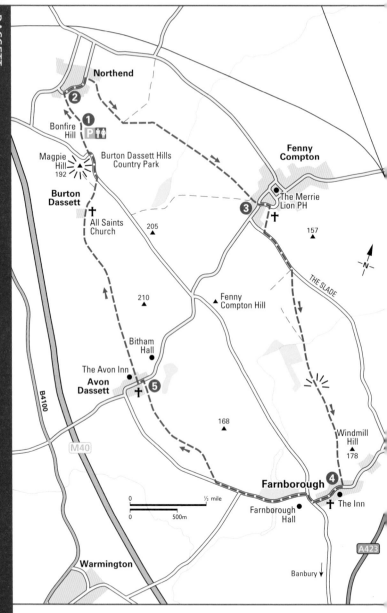

Northend

② ①

Bonfire
Hill 🅿️

Magpie
Hill
192

Burton Dassett Hills
Country Park

Burton
Dassett

✝
All Saints
Church

205 ▲

Fenny
Compton

The Merrie
Lion PH

③

157 ▲

THE SLADE

210 ▲

✝ Fenny
Compton Hill

N

Bitham
Hall

The Avon Inn

Avon
Dassett

✝ ⑤

168 ▲

Windmill
Hill
178 ▲

B4100

M40

Farnborough ④

✝ The Inn

0   ½ mile
0   500m

Farnborough ●
Hall

Warmington

A423

Banbury ↓

① From the car park in the Burton
Dassett Hills Country Park descend
the footpath – the Centenary Way
– to the right of Bonfire Hill with its
conical-roofed stone tower (once a
windmill, converted to a beacon), and
go through a kissing gate onto a track
into the village of Northend.

② Go right along Malthouse Lane,
soon becoming Top Street, in the
village for 300yds (274m), then right
again just past Pype Hayes house
onto a track between gardens. Then,
through a kissing gate, follow the
footpath with its waymark arrows,
heading generally eastwards towards

Fenny Compton, crossing a mixture of pasture and cultivated fields via two kissing gates, three stiles and a footbridge.

❸ Enter Fenny Compton through a gate ahead. Follow a hedged path to Grant's Close and go left into Avon Dassett road. Turn right into Church Street and right onto Dog Lane. Go past Ducketts Cottage and through the gate to the right of the village church. Now bear right and cross over pastureland to a gate in the hedge, onto a road known as The Slade. Go left along this past a large farm barn at the brow of the hill, then right over a footbridge and through a kissing gate into a large cultivated field. Go half left and follow the footpath signs, crossing this field to a second footbridge. Here go left, walk along the field edge, and at the stream bear right alongside to a hedge gap. Cross the field corner and continue beside the hedge. Over a footbridge bear half left to another. At a stile continue ahead to the crest of Windmill Hill, from views of the windmill at Chesterton and the BT Communication tower near Daventry. Descend over farm fields and a hedged footpath into the village of Farnborough, emerging via a hedged path on the main street near The Inn.

❹ Head right along the main street, and bear right past the public entrance gates to Farnborough Hall. Continue up the road to the left, then along the permissive footpath beside the lake, inside the trees. At the end of the woodland continue on a field edge permissive path, to emerge back on the lane via a stile. Continue along the road for 400yds (365m), then go right over a stile and across a couple of cultivated fields into pastureland. Descend to the left of a large barn which brings you to Avon Dassett.

❺ Go left past the Roman Catholic church, and in 75yds (69m) go right up Park Close, passing to the right of The Avon pub and into open countryside. Up to the right is the Bitham Hall. The waymarked footpath, the Centenary Way, hugs the top of fields, crossing a large cultivated field, to arrive in Burton Dassett. Pass the church, go through the kissing gate from the churchyard, and continue up the road to the car park near the Beacon.

WHERE TO EAT AND DRINK The Merrie Lion in Fenny Compton is a popular pub, just up the road from the church. The Inn (formerly the Butchers Arms) is a period building with lots of character and lovely gardens in Farnborough. The Avon Inn has a pleasant outside garden and is situated on the track corner in Avon Dassett.

••••

WHAT TO SEE Visit the Norman All Saints Church in Burton Dassett. Its imposing tower overlooks the battlefield of Edgehill, making it the 'Cathedral of the Hills'. Built on the slope of a hill, the floor climbs from the chancel arch with seven groups of steps.

••••

WHILE YOU'RE THERE You'll pass the National Trust's splendid 18th-century Farnborough Hall on the walk route. The home of the Holbech family for some 300 years, this is a superb honey-coloured stone building with impressive plasterwork, well worth exploring.

Round Draycote Water to Dunchurch

DISTANCE 7 miles (11.3km)	MINIMUM TIME 2hrs 30min	
ASCENT/GRADIENT 164ft (50m) ▲ ▲ ▲	LEVEL OF DIFFICULTY ✦✦✦	

PATHS Reservoir paths and field paths

LANDSCAPE Reservoir in gentle, rolling countryside

SUGGESTED MAP OS Explorer 222 Rugby & Daventry

START/FINISH Grid reference: SP 466691

DOG FRIENDLINESS Dogs not permitted around the perimeter of Draycote Water

PARKING Pay-and-display car park at Draycote Water

PUBLIC TOILETS At the visitor centre

This walk offers the opportunity to explore the largest area of open water in Warwickshire and to visit two nearby historic villages. The impressive Draycote Water reservoir is set in more than 600 acres (243ha) of land and attracts large numbers of wildfowl. Owned by Severn Trent Water, it was completed in 1970 as a pumped storage facility. It's refilled during winter months from the nearby River Leam, thus reducing the risk of local flooding.

GUNPOWDER PLOT AND TREASON

A private house in Dunchurch is now called Guy Fawkes but was formerly The Falcon Inn. It was here that the Gunpowder Plot conspirators sought refuge from justice in 1605, after their failed attempt to assassinate King James I as he visited Parliament. Dunchurch was once a busy coaching village and The Dun Cow is the old coaching inn, conveniently situated at the village crossroads. The historical perspective continues on the village green, where you will see the old stocks and an ancient cross. By the crossroads is a statue commemorating Lord John Scott, a local landowner and sportsman. At the time of his death, he had recently equipped a new boat to investigate some of the problems of deep-sea fishing.

The 14th-century St Peter's Church has a fine tower, a Norman door and a font to match. Set inside folding doors is a monument to Thomas Newcombe, who was 'a printer to three kings' and founded the 17th-century almshouses. These now add an air of old-world charm to the hotchpotch of thatched properties in this pleasant village, which is full of floral colour in the spring and summer.

There's another fine view over the reservoir as you descend into Thurlaston. You'll see attractive thatched cottages as you enter, and pass near to a former windmill (now a private residence). The Church of St Edmund was completed in 1848, originally to house the village school. The site was donated by Lord John Scott (he of the statue by the crossroads). The building was used as a church on Sundays, but accommodation for the schoolmaster was built into the tower. The present bell tower was added later, but the schoolmaster's accommodation remains as a private residence. Bizarrely, the bell rope still passes through one of its rooms.

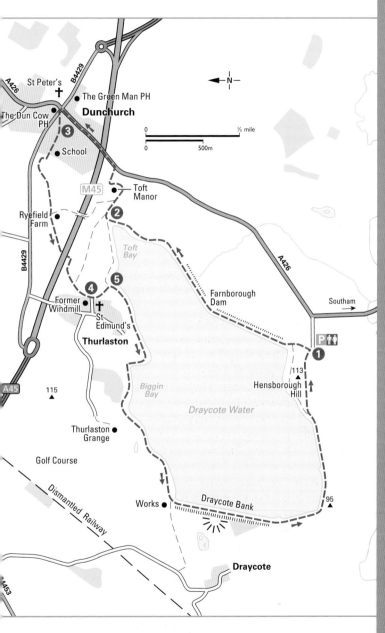

1 From Draycote Water car park proceed up to the reservoir past a sign 'Visitors Centre & Reservoir', and then bear right, following the tarmac lane along the top of Farnborough Dam wall to reach the part of the Water known as Toft Bay.

② At the end of Toft Bay, go right and leave the reservoir grounds via a gate where the perimeter road goes sharp left. Continue ahead for 50 paces, then go right to a gate and follow the waymarker signs to a footpath that climbs past alpaca pens up towards Toft House. Over a stile, bear left along a lane and through a gate. Past Toft Manor, follow the lane round to the right and continue to the A426 Rugby–Dunchurch road. Go left along the road, cross the road bridge and enter the village of Dunchurch, passing a number of attractive thatched properties. The village square and St Peter's Church are to the right of the crossroads, with The Dun Cow pub immediately opposite.

③ At the crossroads go left along the pavement of the B4429 past the Dunchurch Social Club. Bear left along School Street past more thatched properties, and follow a path past the infant school down to the Dunchurch Scout Group Hall. Go right and then left along a footpath to the right of playing fields. The path bears left beside more playing fields to a kissing gate. Continue alongside a hedge, through a gate, and proceed on a track. Cross a lane and go through a kissing gate to the right of Ryefield Farm. Go ahead over pastureland, crossing another lane via two kissing gates, then pass beneath the M45 road bridge via two kissing gates before diagonally crossing the next field to a kissing gate and a handgate through a third gate into Thurlaston.

④ Go to the left by St Edmund's Church and via a gate down a concrete farm track to a kissing gate and a footbridge. Enter the perimeter of Draycote Water via a handgate.

⑤ Go right along the walkway by the side of the reservoir around Biggin Bay. To your right Thurlaston Grange can be seen, and then you will pass a golf course. Continue around the end of the reservoir, passing by the treatment works, and then stroll along Draycote Bank. To your right is the spire of Bourton-on-Dunsmore church about a mile (1.6km) away; to its right is Bourton Hall. After passing the sailing club parking area and just before reaching the yachting area, go right through a gate onto a footpath. This leads via a kissing gate up onto Hensborough Hill. Meander past the trig point, some 371ft (113m) above sea level, the head towards the visitor centre, returning to the car park via a kissing gate.

WHERE TO EAT AND DRINK There are a couple of pubs in Dunchurch. The Green Man is situated along the B4429 Daventry Road. The Dun Cow at the crossroads is a popular eating place for local walkers and welcomes children but not dogs.

● ● ● ●

WHAT TO SEE St Peter's Church and Bourton Hall are local landmarks to the west of Draycote Water and are clearly visible as you walk around the reservoir. Situated on Dunsmore Heath in the village of Bourton-on-Dunsmore, St Peter's has a fine 13th-century font, a Jacobean altar and a ghost in its vestry. The 18th-century Bourton Hall was restored in 1979.

Napton on the Hill's Historic Windmill

DISTANCE 2.5 miles (4km)	MINIMUM TIME 1hr 15min

ASCENT/GRADIENT 213ft (65m) ▲▲▲   LEVEL OF DIFFICULTY ✦✦✦

PATHS Field paths, farm tracks and country lanes

LANDSCAPE Rolling Warwickshire countryside

SUGGESTED MAP OS Explorers 206 Edge Hill & Fenny Compton; 222 Rugby & Daventry

START/FINISH Grid reference: SP 463612

DOG FRIENDLINESS Off lead along tow path, otherwise under control

PARKING St Lawrence's Church car park, Napton on the Hill

PUBLIC TOILETS None on route

This walk takes you over Napton Hill and past its historic windmill, with its unmoving arms outstretched against the skyline. On a good day you can see seven counties from the windswept summit. Apparently, during World War II, the locals sat at the top of the hill to watch the bombing of Coventry and its surrounding area.

MILL ON THE HILL

There has been a windmill at Napton on the Hill since 1543 – it is one of the great landmarks in Warwickshire. Next to the privately owned mill building is the former miller's stone cottage, which still houses parts of the original bread oven. Early maps of the area reveal that there were once two windmills on the hill. They drew a regular and pure supply of water from underground springs and wells. The present windmill is in good condition but not open to the public.

INDUSTRIAL REVOLUTION

The village of Napton on the Hill, whose name derives from the old British word 'cnapton', meaning 'farm on the knap of the hill', was a substantial settlement in 1086. It was granted a charter in 1321 to hold a weekly market and an annual fair, and became a prosperous medieval village. Today, attractive mellowed brown and gold thatched houses contribute to a picturesque scene.

You could be forgiven for thinking this was a timeless image, untouched by the revolutionary industrial changes which were taking place elsewhere in the West Midlands, but even Napton succumbed to 'canal mania' towards the end of the 18th century. Britain was gripped as the whole country clamoured to invest in the new transport technology. In a two-year period in the 1790s, 37 separate Acts of Parliament were passed to enable the construction of an amazing system of 4,250 miles (6,840km) of navigable rivers and canals. The Oxford Canal, completed in 1790, was part of this and it encouraged canalside businesses to develop. Workmen were more than happy to take alcohol at The Folly Inn while they laboured in the construction of the flight of seven Napton Locks.

A VERY PECULIAR CHURCH

The 12th-century St Lawrence's Church, on the brow of the hill, was originally going to be built at the bottom of the hill, and the stone was assembled there, ready for its construction. Overnight, however, the stone was mysteriously moved to the present site, near the top of the hill – and the church was erected where it lay.

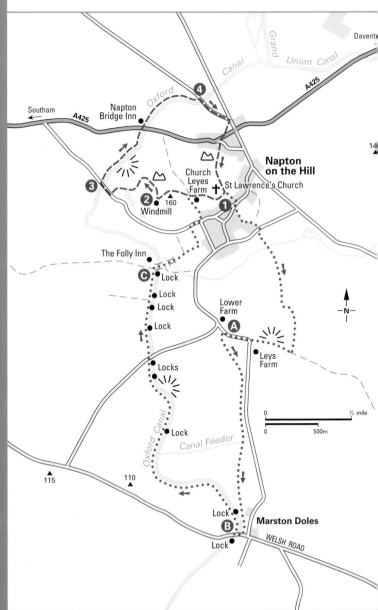

1 From the car park, walk around the outside of the churchyard of St Lawrence's Church and pass by a smaller car park. From here take the track that becomes a lane and pass by Church Leyes Farm. At the lane junction, go ahead and follow the driveway towards the superb windmill which comes into view – the building and its land are private, so please respect the 'Private' signs and keep off the property.

2 Reaching wooden gates, go right along a footpath around the outside of the property, following the waymarkers. Through a gate this leads to lovely open land, and you now can go downhill, following the path that descends beside a fence line. After crossing a stile, continue steeply downhill. The path then bears sharp left and leads you past a fishing pool. Keep by the fence to reach the lane by the side of Tilehurst house, Brickyard Lane. Go right down the lane and cross bridge No. 112 over the Oxford Canal.

3 Over the bridge, descend right onto the tow path, go through a gate and then walk to the left by the canal. This is easy, pleasant walking with great views up to your right of Napton Hill with its windmill on top.

4 Leave the tow path at bridge No. 110 via a gate, and walk up the lane back towards the village. Just before a road junction, go right over a stile and cross the corner of a field to a further stile onto the A425 road. Bear right and cross the main road and a road called Hillside, then go through a waymarked gate and begin to climb the hill up a clear, hedged footpath. As you approach the top of the hill the path becomes less steep and you will go through two metal kissing gates and two bridle gates to reach open land once again. To your right you will see St Lawrence's Church. Go right along the church lane back to your car to complete the walk.

WHERE TO EAT AND DRINK The walk route passes two public houses which welcome walkers. The Bridge at Napton is situated on the A425 as you reach the Oxford Canal. It offers good food and fine canalside gardens. The Folly Inn (Folly 'Pie Pub') serves traditional food. It stands by Napton Bottom Lock and is filled with charming bygones.

WHAT TO SEE Visit St Lawrence's Church whose squat tower has, like the windmill, withstood centuries of buffeting from the wind. The north door is called the Devil's Door and used to be opened during baptisms for the Devil to escape. At Christmas or other festivals you may hear the ringing of hand bells. Inside there is a slate portrait of John Shuckburgh of nearby Shuckburgh Hall.

WHILE YOU'RE THERE A visit to the Nickelodeon Museum is an amazing experience. It once occupied the old Methodist chapel in Napton, but the number of organs grew too large and it has been moved to Ashorne Hall, about 12 miles (19.3km) to the west of here. It's a remarkable working collection of vintage juke-boxes, symphoniums and many other exotic musical machines.

A Circuit from Napton via the Oxford Canal

DISTANCE 6.5 miles (10.4km)   MINIMUM TIME 2hrs

ASCENT/GRADIENT 427ft (130m) ▲▲▲   LEVEL OF DIFFICULTY +++

SEE MAP AND INFORMATION PANEL FOR WALK 48

From Napton on the Hill this walk ventures into attractive, open countryside offering extensive views. The route includes a longer stretch of tow path along the Oxford Canal, passing several locks and giving the opportunity to visit The Folly Inn.

Cross the church lane at Point ❶ and proceed on the path ahead, descending to Vicarage Road. Head right along the main road for 50yds (46m), then go left down Godsons Lane. At the road junction go right along Dog Lane. Go right for 50yds (46m), then left , just before the school sign, along a hedged bridleway, heading southeast away from Napton.

Continue in this direction for about 350yds (320m), then ahead, passing through a series of farm gates. After the third one, go left alongside the hedge, through another field gate, then sharp right alongside a hedge. Reach a field gate at a track and go right (enjoy the fine retrospective view of Napton on the Hill). Reach a final farm gate to the right of farm buildings – Leys Farm is further to the left. Go ahead along the road, passing Lower Farm (Point Ⓐ). Just before the junction of roads by the 40mph sign, go left over a stile and follow the waymarker direction as you cross the field diagonally left, heading southeast. In the next field head for a stile in a wire fence, then continue to a stile in the hedge ahead and walk parallel with the road hedge, going southwards. Continue over several fields and two stiles, passing to the left of a canal feeder and a derelict building, then cross meadowland via a stile until you come to Welsh Road, via a final gate, near to Marston Doles (Point Ⓑ).

Cross canal bridge No. 119 and go left, via a gate, to the tow path and turn left under the bridge. Walk along the tow path of the Oxford Canal, heading north towards Napton. Continue past the lock gates. Just after bridge No. 116, there is an exceptional view of Napton. Continue along the tow path to bridge No. 113, where you can visit The Folly Inn (Point Ⓒ).

Cross the bridge into Folly Lane. In 50yds (46m), go left over a stile and continue over meadowland to cross a footbridge, then proceed ahead along a short stretch of track to a stile. Follow the direction of the waymarker to another stile, and cross the large field diagonally to a final stile onto Poplar Road. Go right along the road for 80yds (73m), then left opposite Howcombe Lane junction. This leads back to the lane junction close to Church Leyes Farm. At the junction, go right and return to the car park at St Lawrence's Church (Point ❶).

Harborough Magna

DISTANCE 3.5 miles (5.7km)	MINIMUM TIME 1hr 45min

ASCENT/GRADIENT 49ft (15m) ▲▲▲   LEVEL OF DIFFICULTY ✚✚✚

PATHS Field footpaths and tow path

LANDSCAPE Gentle countryside

SUGGESTED MAP OS Explorer 222 Rugby & Daventry

START/FINISH Grid reference: SP 478792

DOG FRIENDLINESS Off lead along tow path, otherwise under control

PARKING Village streets near The Old Lion pub or, with permission, the pub car park

PUBLIC TOILETS None on route

This walk starts from The Old Lion pub in Harborough Magna and crosses farmland into the village of Easenhall, which comprises a small number of houses, the 17th-century Golden Lion Hotel and a couple of farms. Further pastureland is walked on the way to the Oxford Canal. From here, a short stretch of tow path leads to more farmland walking on the return journey to Harborough Magna.

GREATER AND SMALLER

Situated some 4 miles (6.4km) north of Rugby, Harborough Magna is an old village which embraces the hamlets of Harborough Parva and Cathiron. The name Harborough appears to derive from the Saxon English 'heord beorg', meaning 'the hill where flocks are kept'. Its Latinised suffix Magna (Great) was added to distinguish the village from similarly named settlements near by (Parva means 'little' in this context).

There was a priest and a mill here when William I's Domesday surveyors entered the parish in their records. Much later, the village also boasted a smithy and a wheelwright, where carts were constructed and repaired for use at the timber yards of William Iven. The whole area seems to have been involved in this industry at some time. Saw mills were located at Cathiron, near to the Oxford Canal, and the timber was transported via cart and canal barge to the saw mills. Plenty of cart horses were kept locally, and teams of horses could be seen hauling the larger trees from the nearby estates to Rugby Station, where they were trimmed and cut in readiness for transportation. With the demise of the industry, pleasure boats have now taken over the Oxford Canal.

EASENHALL

Easenhall is a quaint old village of cottages and semi-detached Victorian houses. In the past these housed workers belonging to the Manor House at Newbold Revel. The route passes next to the old chapel – a small, one-room former Congregational building, now the village hall.

To the southwest of the villages the route crosses the West Coast Main Line, formerly the London Midland Railway that runs from Euston to Glasgow, now at high speeds with colourful express trains flashing by. Before the War, prestige expresses such as the streamlined *Coronation Scot* or trains of maroon coaches hauled by Sir William Stanier's great pacific locomotives covered the footbridge watchers in sooty steam.

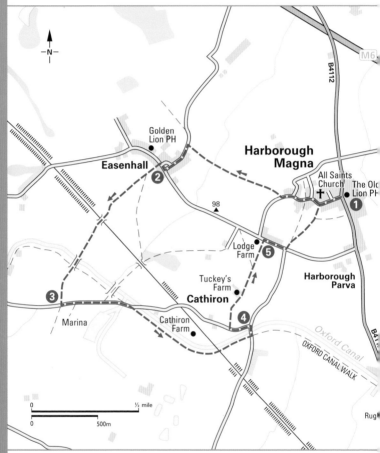

❶ From the car park of The Old Lion pub, cross the B4112 and head up Main Street and into the village. Walk past All Saints Church, noting its unique clock face, and continue to the end of the village. Twenty five paces after passing by Holly Cottage, go right over a stile and follow the footpath across cultivated fields towards Easenhall, climbing another stile. Cross a footbridge to reach the village, via another stile, near the thatched Campbell's Cottage. Go left through the village down to a junction of roads by the village green, with the building of the former chapel facing you. The Golden Lion public house, restaurant and hotel is to the right-hand side, and to the left you will see a painted, weatherboarded house called Brooklands.

❷ Cross the road and proceed up a hedged footpath to the right of The Chapel House, and after negotiating a handgate and a kissing gate you will come to open countryside. Continue in a southwesterly direction and through a kissing gate, following a path heading towards a prominent footbridge over the main line railway. Cross the footbridge and walk ahead over the next field. Cross bridge No. 37 of the Oxford Canal, and continue ahead across pasture and beyond another kissing gate, arriving on a lane, via a gate.

❸ Go left along the lane for about 600yds (549m) until you come to bridge No. 41, where there is an easy descent via steps onto the tow path of this peaceful canal. Here you are joining the Oxford Canal Walk and you go right along the tow path, past Cathiron Farm (on the far bank). Pass under the railway line, and at bridge No. 43 (Tuckey's Bridge), ascend onto a lane. Cross the bridge and go left at the lane junction.

❹ In 160yds (146m), go right through a handgate and follow the drive heading north towards Tuckey's Farm. Go through the gate on the right two thirds of the way up the drive, and head to another to the right of the farm complex. Cross a drive via another handgate and continue over the next field and through a kissing gate in the hedge, aiming towards houses. Leave the field via a kissing gate and footbridge onto the Easenhall Road, with Lodge Farm on your left.

❺ Go right along the road, passing a row of houses. Opposite the Cathiron Road junction, go left and take the hedged footpath. Through a kissing gate, briefly follow the hedge and then head diagonally to the far corner of the field, aiming towards a metal kissing gate. Through this cross a footbridge and pass through another kissing gate. Cross the next field to a kissing gate by a grey house, bringing you back to Main Street in Harborough Magna. Go right along Main Street, then cross the B4112 back to The Old Lion.

WHERE TO EAT AND DRINK The walk starts from the car park at The Old Lion in Harborough Magna, which is a popular venue for local walkers. In the village of Easenhall you will pass near the appealing Golden Lion Hotel, with its part wattle-and-daub walls.

● ● ● ●

WHAT TO SEE If you intend walking around the lanes of Easenhall after dark, beware and look out for the Phantom Horseman. He is apparently the ghost of a one-handed man called Broughton who died in Old Lawford Hall. Legend has it that, in an attempt to exorcise his ghost, his remains were placed in a phial and tossed into a nearby pond.

● ● ● ●

WHILE YOU'RE THERE A little further down the canal, Newbold Quarry country park is well worth a diversion. There is a car park which can be reached via Yates Avenue, off the A426. The lake attracts wading birds and ducks, and beneath the surface are crayfish. In the park surrounds you will find lime-loving plants and wild flowers in abundance, as well as many species of butterflies.

Titles in the Series

- 50 Walks in Berkshire and Buckinghamshire
- 50 Walks in the Brecon Beacons and South Wales
- 50 Walks in Cambridgeshire and the East Midlands
- 50 Walks in Cornwall
- 50 Walks in the Cotswolds
- 50 Walks in Derbyshire
- 50 Walks in Devon
- 50 Walks in Dorset
- 50 Walks in Durham and Northumberland
- 50 Walks in Edinburgh and Eastern Scotland
- 50 Walks in Essex
- 50 Walks in Glasgow and South West Scotland
- 50 Walks in Gloucestershire
- 50 Walks in Hampshire and the Isle of Wight
- 50 Walks in Herefordshire and Worcestershire
- 50 Walks in Hertfordshire
- 50 Walks in Kent
- 50 Walks in the Lake District
- 50 Walks in Lancashire and Cheshire
- 50 Walks in London
- 50 Walks in Norfolk
- 50 Walks in North Yorkshire
- 50 Walks in Oxfordshire
- 50 Walks in the Peak District
- 100 Walks in Scotland
- 50 Walks in the Scottish Highlands and Islands
- 50 Walks in Shropshire
- 50 Walks in Snowdonia and North Wales
- 50 Walks in Somerset
- 50 Walks in Staffordshire
- 50 Walks in Suffolk
- 50 Walks in Surrey
- 50 Walks in Sussex
- 50 Walks in Warwickshire and West Midlands
- 50 Walks in West Yorkshire
- 50 Walks in Wiltshire
- 50 Walks in the Yorkshire Dales